GREEN COMMUTER PLANS: DO THEY WORK?

Tom Rye and David McGuigan

Napier University Transport Research Unit

Scottish Executive Central Research Unit
2000

The views expressed in this report are those of the researchers. They do not necessarily represent those of the Department or Scottish Ministers.

CONTENTS

ACKNOWLEDGEMENTS

The authors would like to recognise the contribution of the following to this report.

To Steve Potter, for his input throughout. For her general assistance and input on the early stages of the project, Fran Alston.

Hewlett Packard

To Michael McBride and Ian McIntosh for their untiring support and helpfulness in arranging meetings and providing information.

To all the HP staff who took part in interviews, focus groups, SP interviews and filled in their travel surveys.

To Nazan Çelikel, Hersham Fawzy, Dr.Wafaa Saleh and David Seaman for their respective input to the design, piloting, carrying out and analysis of the SP surveys at HP.

Kirkton Campus

To Ben Ireland for his initial work on Green Travel issues at the campus.

To John Bennett of West Lothian Chamber of Commerce and Alistair Short and Roy Mitchell of West Lothian Council for their significant role in carrying out the Kirkton Campus Travel surveys, and for convening and running the Kirkton Campus Commuter Forum.

To those employees and managers at the Royal Bank of Scotland Statement Dispatch Centre, Quintiles and B.SkyB who took part in focus groups and interviews.

Gyle/New Edinburgh Park

To Caryll Paterson (convener) and all member organisations of the Gyle/NEP Employer Travel Planning Focus Group for allowing the history of their activities, including travel survey data, to be included in this report.

To Iain Fairgrieve, David Graham and David Mathie at the Royal Bank of Scotland for their assistance with setting up focus groups and taking the time to be interviewed about the RBS' green travel initiatives.

To staff at Safeway, the Royal Bank and at Scottish Equitable for taking part in focus groups.

To Gordon Paterson, New Edinburgh Park Management, for his assistance and provision of information.

In addition, the report draws on interviews with HSBC Call Centre and with New Edinburgh Park Management in early 1999 as part of the DETR Project *"The Costs and Benefits of Green Commuter Plans"*. This project was carried out by Oscar Faber, Napier University and the Open University.

SUMMARY

A Green Commuter Plan (GCP)[1] is a package of measures implemented by employers to reduce the proportion of their staff driving alone to, from and at work. The aims of this 18 month research project were to:

- Examine the potential and actual contribution of GCPs to achieving modal shift
- Identify the factors which make GCPs successful
- Determine the most effective elements of GCPs
- Identify barriers to GCP implementation, and ways to overcome these

To do this, three case study sites were chosen: Hewlett Packard (HP), (now Agilent Technologies), a single employer in South Queensferry, near Edinburgh; the South Gyle/New Edinburgh Park (NEP) employment area in West Edinburgh; and the Kirkton Campus business park in Livingston. These sites were chosen because, while all of them were undertaking some form of GCP activity, they were all very much at different stages of GCP development. Furthermore, they provided a contrast between single employer GCPs and employers working together. Some details of the case study sites are presented in the Table below.

Table i.1 – Comparison of site characteristics

	HP	Gyle/NEP	Kirkton Campus
Location	Edge of small town 8 miles northwest of Edinburgh	Western edge of Edinburgh	1.5 miles west of Livingston Town Centre, W. Lothian
Number of employers	1	Approx 20	Approx 50
Number of employees	1500	12000	8000
% commuting alone by car	59	72	64
Road access	Excellent though Forth Bridge congested at peak times	Excellent off-peak, heavily congested at peak	Excellent
Public transport access	Rail: good to central Edinburgh and Fife Bus: poor	Rail: good to central Edinburgh and Fife Bus: good to central Edinburgh, moderate to West Lothian, very poor orbital links	Rail: poor Bus: poor – half hourly frequencies or worse, most services require change at Livingston Centre
GCP in place	Yes	Varies by company	No
Transport problems	Parking, on-site congestion	Parking (varies by company), on- and off-site congestion	No, with the exception of parking and congestion related to B.Sky.B

---

[1] The UK Government Transport Minister announced in January 2000 that GCPs will henceforth be known as Travel Plans. However, for the purposes of this project, the earlier parlance is used.

Whilst not all of the project objectives were fully achieved, the research has answered the question "Green Commuter Plans – Do They Work?" with a qualified "yes". Two case study organisations in this project achieved a significant reduction in the proportion of their staff driving alone to work as a result of a GCP. At HP, the proportion of staff driving alone fell from 65% in 1997 to 59% in 1999. At the Royal Bank of Scotland in the Gyle/NEP, the proportion of staff carsharing to work rose from about 25% to roughly 35%.

At an early stage of the project, a model of GCP development was introduced to conceptualise this process. This posits that organisations can be at any one of the following stages:

- **Pre-contemplation** – here, the organisation may be unaware of the idea of GCPs
- **Contemplation** – here, some change in the internal or external environment leads the organisation to begin thinking about GCPs and their implications
- **Preparation** – here, the organisation begins to plan and prepare their GCP
- **Action**, at which stage measures to manage employee travel are actually implemented. This can be further divided into:
  - **Basic** (and low cost) measures such as public transport information, cycle facilities and car-sharing schemes
  - **Incentives** – measures that may impose a financial or organisational cost, such as public transport subsidies, or compressed work weeks
  - **Disincentives** – principally parking management and changes in eligibility for travel allowances
- **Maintenance** – here the plan is monitored, up-dated and maintained.

At any stage, an organisation may relapse from one stage to another, earlier stage.

Most organisations in the Kirkton Campus case study site were at the pre-contemplation or contemplation stage when this study began. At the Gyle/NEP, they were on a continuum from contemplation to action. HP was at the most advanced stage of the model, maintenance.

The main methodologies used for the research project were:
- Travel surveys, to establish baseline travel patterns and, at HP, to measure changes.
- Panel interviews and surveys with a small group of staff at selected sites, to obtain more information on travel behaviour and attitudes to GCPs.
- Focus groups.
- Structured interviews with key management staff to understand organisational attitudes to GCPs.
- Stated preference work at HP, to understand how staff might react, were additional GCP measures to be introduced.

Hewlett Packard

At Hewlett Packard, the GCP was implemented for a number of reasons:

- General environmental concerns/social responsibility
- Specific health and safety concerns regarding the site car park circulation and capacity, particularly in the context of a large increase in employee numbers in 1996-7 and again in 2000
- To reduce the risk of overspill parking on local streets
- To offer employees greater choice of modes to work

The main components of the GCP are low cost and low intervention, as follows:

- Cycle parking, showers and lockers
- Preferential parking for carsharers with 3 or more in the team; a carshare database to promote carpool formation
- A discount of up to 40% on rail season tickets to Dalmeny station (adjacent to the site) negotiated with and paid for by the train operator Scotrail
- Promotion of and information about alternative modes
- The phasing out of company perk cars and their replacement with clean-fuelled pool vehicles

Interviews with senior management revealed that they were happy to keep the GCP at this level but would be unlikely to commit further significant resources to it, unless there were changes in the external environment (such as introduction of the PNR parking levy). Thus a full cost benefit evaluation of or business case for the GCP was not seen to be necessary. HP implemented its GCP in 1997 in tandem with expansion of on-site car parking and further increases in staff numbers in 2000 are being dealt with using a similar "two-pronged" approach.

A staff travel survey carried out in 1997 and replicated in 1999 found a statistically significant modal shift: the proportion of staff driving alone fell from 65% to 59% due to an increase in rail use from 8 to 14%. The proportion of staff carsharing also fell. The 1999 survey also found that most staff rated the GCP measures as ineffective, with the exception of the rail discount.

The stated preference survey at HP revealed that measures combining disincentives to car use (parking charges) and significant incentives for carsharing and public transport could encourage a further 25% of drive alone staff to convert to a different mode. However, as noted above, such measures are unlikely to be implemented in the near future.

The significance of the travel survey results from HP should not be underestimated. They are an important addition to very limited before and after monitoring data for GCPs in the UK. However, it remains to be seen if this achievement can be built on without greater expenditure of resources by the company in the future.

Kirkton Campus

The Kirkton Campus business park was included in the project because the local Council, West Lothian, wished to promote such activity to reduce the risk of (future) congestion compromising the accessibility of this important employment area. This was particularly related to a major inward investment by a US Computer company, Cadence. However, at present, congestion in the area is limited to the shift changeover times of B.Sky.B, by far the largest local employer. Other employers have few problems with on site congestion or parking.

Initial awareness raising on GCPs was carried out by a consultant to the Council, who wrote to all firms and visited major employers to assess their interest. An attempt was made to form a Kirkton Campus Green Commuting Forum; when a chair from one of the organisations in the campus was not forthcoming, the local Chamber of Commerce played this role. The Forum met four times and distributed staff travel surveys and results, as well as public transport information. After the first Forum meeting, attendance was very poor. Organisations did not appear ready to contribute to the initiative or to work together on transport issues.

A staff travel survey was carried out with 17 firms in the Campus. The overall response rate was approximately 5%. The results are shown below:

Table i.2 Usual mode of travel by number, percentage and average distance				
Mode	Number	%	UK 1996 mode, %	Distance, Kirkton
Car, on your own.	286	64		14.6
Car, passenger.	63	14	70	6.3
Car, sharing.	48	11		9.8
Bus.	25	6	8	9.0
Other: Minibus.	14	3	-	9.6
Bicycle.	7	2	4	5.9
Walk.	5	1	12	1.8
Other: Bus then lift.	1	0	2	8.6
Train.	1	0	3	14.7
Missing.	1	0	-	-
All modes	**451**	**100**		**12.2**

Interviews and focus groups in selected organisations revealed an extremely poor perception of local public transport services, and a low organisational priority attached to green commuting. Where staff did not have cars available, the usual alternative was to carshare and, at certain employers, this was found to be very widespread.

Since the research was carried out, local bus services have improved, as a new employer in the campus (the Halifax) has paid for a new bus service to the main town centre and bus service in Livingston. The Council has also produced a new Kirkton Campus public transport information leaflet. However, Kirkton Campus remains, mostly, at pre-contemplation/contemplation stage in the model of GCP development.

Gyle/New Edinburgh Park (NEP)

Certain Gyle/NEP employers have worked together on GCP issues since November 1998, when they formed a Travel Forum that continued to meet every 6 weeks to May 2000. This is because, although they have individual problems with parking and transport (to varying degrees), they also recognised that these problems are in part shared and therefore require joint solutions. At the same time individual employers have developed their own GCPs. Details of the employers on the Forum are shown in Table i.3, below; this is not an exhaustive list of companies in the area, however, since membership of the group is voluntary. It is the case that certain employers on the Forum have been much more active than others. The Royal Bank has been subject to acute parking problems and so has put most resources into GCP measures, with significant results; the management company in NEP has also been very active because the site is still expanding and subject to planning conditions relating to transport.

The joint activities of the group have included:

- Data gathering/sharing
- Lobbying PT providers, which has resulted in improved services to the City Centre
- Lobbying the local Council for better parking control
- Attending meetings of the Forum
- However, there has <u>not</u> been any joint funding services or other measures as yet (May 2000).

Individual employers' GCPs include, or have included:

- Discount bus tickets and PT promotion
- Car-sharing and (at one) linked parking management
- Cycle facilities
- Company bus services

The Gyle/NEP shows that joint working on GCPs has some benefits but that companies with a problem will continue to work alone even if there is no joint action. Where a management company acts on behalf of many organisations, there is more scope for effective area-wide initiatives.

Table i.3 Gyle Employers

	Royal Bank		Bank of Scotland		Gyle Centre	Scottish Courage		HSBC	Scottish Equitable		BT	Marks and Spencer		Scottish Provident	Other NEP		TOTAL	
	n	%	n	%	n	N	%	n	n	%	n	n	%	n	n	%	n	%
Current employees	1600		1753		100	360		494	2364			380			850		7901	
Projected employees	2500		1800		100	360		700	2500		900	380		100			9340	
Parking spaces (ratio)	1160	.73	674	.38		165	.46	280	1200	.51		70	.18				3549	.45
Responses	1353		823			87			1790			145			504		4702	
Travel survey % response rate		84.5		47			24			76			38			59.2		60%
Work times																		
arrive 8 – 9	989	73.1				65	72											
leave 5 – 6	875	64.7																
Commute mode																		
solo car	907	67.0	708	86.0		58	66.7		1269	70.9		78	53.8		353	70.0	3373	71.7
carshare	235	17.4	49	6.0		16	18.4		511	28.5		0	0.0		50	9.9	.862	18.3
bus	238	17.6	49	6.0		1	1.1		132	7.4		39	26.9		66	13.1	525	11.2
train	95	7.0	8	1.0		8	9.2					10	6.9		10	2.0	131	2.8
Alternative modes																		
consider bus	409	30.2	247	30.0											121	24.0	777	16.5
consider train/CERT	310	22.9	181	22.0											71	14.1	562	12.0
consider carshare	860	63.6				40			577								1477	31.4

Gaps in this table are because data has not been collected from respective companies

Conclusion

This project has shown that GCPs can work, and make a significant contribution to modal shift at the site level. At the network level, however, the impact is much less clear. GCPs also have an awareness raising impact that may contribute to modal shift.

The factors that contribute to the success of GCPs are, firstly and most importantly, a site specific problem with congestion, parking and/or transport-related staff recruitment. Additionally, a supportive organisational culture can be of great benefit, as can staff dedicated to the GCP. Joint work between organisations has also been shown to be of some use in raising awareness, building morale amongst transport staff in companies, and lobbying public transport providers.

The most effective measures that go to make up a GCP vary from site to site (e.g. HP's rail promotion would have been useless, had the site not been adjacent to a station) and, for maximum effect, should include carrots and sticks, as at the Royal Bank of Scotland. The promotion, as well as the nature of the measure, is also key.

There are barriers to GCP implementation, but these can be overcome. Marketing by organisations and by public transport operators *can* improve often poor perceptions of alternative modes. In certain types of organisation, a rational and technical approach that identifies the costs and benefits of GCPs, can pay dividends in gaining management support, which is critical. However, a GCP may never be needed in the first place if the organisation locates in the right place with appropriate (public transport) infrastructure and reduced parking – at nodal points in the public transport network, for example.

> The research shows that the biggest barrier to the implementation of GCPs is the organisation's perception that there is no problem with transport or parking. The choice for policy makers is, therefore, whether they wish to "create such conditions" through planning control on new development, parking taxes or traffic restraint.

Further research should carry out a full "after" travel survey at the Royal Bank. It should also address the issue of the network effects of GCPs. Finally and most importantly it should address the legality and feasibility of "creating such conditions" by requiring GCPs in new development through the planning process.

1. CHAPTER ONE

1.1 Introduction

This is the final report produced for the 17 month research project "Green Commuter Plans: Do They Work?", which has been carried out for the Scottish Executive Central Research Unit and funded by the DETR.

This report presents details of work carried out to monitor the development, implementation and effects of Green Commuter Plans (GCPs) at Hewlett Packard, South Queensferry; at the Kirkton Campus business park in Livingston; and in the Gyle/New Edinburgh Park business parks in west Edinbugh. These different sites were chosen because they are at different stages in a model of GCP development: when this research project commenced, Hewlett Packard had already implemented its GCP, the Gyle/NEP were in the initial planning stages, and in Kirkton Campus, most organisations were not aware of the concept.

It should be noted at this stage that in January 2000, the English Transport Minister John Prescott decided that Green Commuter Plans should henceforth be known as Travel Plans (TPs). Given that the majority of this Scottish Executive project was carried out prior to the change in terminology, the term Green Commuter Plan (GCP) continues to be used throughout; however, the term is synonymous with Travel Plan.

It should also be noted that in September 1999 Hewlett Packard South Queensferry changed its name to Agilent Technologies. This did not however affect its internal structure, the number of employees based at the site, nor its corporate culture. For the remainder of the report, therefore, the company will be referred to as HP.

1.2 Study Objectives

The objectives of this study are to:

- Examine the potential and actual contribution of GCPs to achieving modal shift
- To identify the factors which make GCPs successful
- To determine the most effective elements of GCPs
- To identify barriers to GCP implementation, and ways to overcome these

The subsequent chapters address these objectives, although to a different degree in each case study, due largely to the state of development of green travel initiatives at each site. The methodology employed to explore these objectives includes:

- Visits to employers at Kirkton Campus, carried out by Ben Ireland Consultants during November 1998
- Minutes of the meetings of the Kirkton Campus Green Commuter Forum
- Interviews with senior managers at 3 Campus organisations
- Focus groups with employees at the same 3 organisations
- Data from Hewlett Packard's (HP) 1997 and 1999 staff travel surveys

- Observation of meetings
- Review of original documents where available
- Interviews with HP managers
- Further surveys of a panel of HP staff
- Interviews with this panel of staff
- Focus groups with HP staff
- Minutes of the meetings of the Gyle/NEP Employers' Travel Planning Focus Group.
- Staff travel surveys from the Bank of Scotland, Royal Bank of Scotland and Scottish Equitable.
- Focus groups with staff at Scottish Equitable, the Royal Bank and Safeway.

The HP panel, of approximately 50 employees, was not intended to be a statistically representative sample of employees, but was rather a body of respondents who were surveyed regularly to assess changes over time in attitudes and behaviour relating to the GCP. This increased the research team's ability to relate the results of the 1997 staff travel survey to those of a further full staff travel survey which took place in November 1999

Chapter Two presents a brief history of Green Commuter Planning and explains some of the reasons why organisations decide to implement GCPs. Chapter Three reports back on research carried out at the Hewlett Packard case study site, where the GCP was in operation prior to the commencement of this project. In particular, it presents results of interviews with key staff who have been involved in the development of the GCP at HP, presents a short analysis of the impacts of HP's strong corporate culture on the plan's evolution, and reports back on two staff travel surveys which have been carried out. It further presents the results of panel interviews and focus groups, and a comparison of the 1997 and 1999 staff travel surveys.

Chapter Four reports on the steps taken towards the development of a Green Commuter Forum among the employers at the Kirkton Campus in West Lothian, and provides the results of a staff travel survey, interviews and focus groups with employers on the campus. Chapter Five gives a history of green commuting initiatives among employers in West Edinburgh's Gyle/NEP employment area, using similar survey material to that gathered in Kirkton Campus. (While this area was not originally planned to be a case study for this report, it was added latterly due to a lack of progress on implementation in Kirkton Campus. The reasons for this are discussed in Chapter Four.) Finally, Chapter Six draws some key conclusions about the work carried out, attempts to relate these to the overall research objectives, makes recommendations for further research work, and gives policy recommendations for the further implementation of Green Commuter Plans.

The reader should note that two Interim Reports were produced for this project, covering initial survey work at HP and at Kirkton Campus. Not all the information in the Interim Reports is reproduced here; for access to these, the interested reader should contact the Scottish Executive Central Research Unit.

2. CHAPTER TWO

2.1 History of Green Commuter Planning

This section of the report explains why organisations implement GCPs, and also presents a model of their development which aids understanding of the processes which are currently underway at HP and at Kirkton Campus. It should be noted that this Chapter is taken largely from a draft report to the DETR (London) on the Costs and Benefits of Green Commuter Plans; it is presented here in its entirety due to its relevance to the Scottish project.

2.2 What is a Green Commuter Plan?

'Green Commuter Plan' (GCP) is the generic term used to encompass initiatives to encourage the use of alternatives to the car and to manage car-use, in order to reduce the environmental impacts of transport. A GCP provides a strategy for an organisation to reduce its transportation impacts and to influence the travel behaviour of its employees, suppliers, visitors and customers. The adoption of GCPs by employers in the UK is an important element of the Government's integrated transport strategy outlined in the 1998 Transport White Paper, 'A New Deal for transport: Better for Everyone'. The Scottish White Paper, 'Travel Choices for Scotland', was published shortly after and also features GCPs by employers as an important element of transport policy for Scotland.

A GCP can incorporate a range of transport-related initiatives to address different transport aspects, including commuter journeys (specifically devised to manage travel to and from the workplace), business travel (all journeys made in the course of the working day), and fleet management (lorries, company cars). The elements of a GCP are varied. It can incorporate a broad package of complementary measures, depending on the objectives and targets set.

2.3 Background

It is useful here to outline briefly the history of the concept of GCPs. Although, GCPs are relatively new in the UK, transportation plans for an organisation have been evident in the US since the late 1970s and early 1980s. Initially, the main focus was to promote car sharing and vanpool schemes to alleviate recruitment and retention issues associated with long journeys to work. In the late 1980s local authorities in areas of high economic growth recognised the demand management potential of GCPs and began to require these be implemented in new developments.

Interest in GCPs emerged in Europe in the mid-1980s. The Netherlands Ministry of Transport implemented GCP measures as a method of reducing traffic congestion. In 1989 targets for the adoption of GCPs were included in the Second National Structure Plan. Within six years all employers with 50 employees were required to have their own GCP.

The initial schemes in the UK emerged from interest in the Dutch initiative in the early 1990s. Nottingham County Council was one of the first organisations to adopt a GCP and since then a number of public and private sector organisations have developed GCPs. In the US implementation has been encouraged through government legislation, such as that governing air quality in Southern California. Whereas in the Netherlands implementation has primarily been on a voluntary basis, guided by government requirements. Currently in the UK there are no government regulations to require organisations to have a GCP.

2.4 GCP development in the UK

In the UK the impetus to develop a GCP has primarily emerged from a number of main motivating factors:

2.4.1 Estate management, accessibility and amenity

To date, in the UK, impetus has largely come from estate management issues. This encompasses a range of site specific problems including parking difficulties, access and egress issues, and accessibility and congestion problems.

A significant incentive to develop and implement a GCP is the need to address a parking problem. In some cases the space or funds for increasing capacity are simply unavailable, in other cases a GCP is considered a much more cost-effective solution to the parking problem. This is especially the case with cash-starved organisations, such as hospitals. Some organisations have a vested interest in attempting to minimise their parking requirements in order that the land can be used for more commercially viable purposes.

Another factor associated with efficient estate management is accessibility. This is a major issue for organisations who depend on customers having good access to the site. For example, airports, retail parks and business parks. It is also a key factor for organisations served by goods vehicles, such as manufacturers, and for hospitals who need to ensure emergency vehicles can access the site unobstructed.

In addition to the site-specific issues, accessibility and amenity around the site can be made poorer by traffic. This affects not just the employer and employers but also and significantly the wider local community.

2.4.2 External regulation

Planning regulations are an increasingly common motivator for GCP development in the UK. One of the most useful tools to encourage GCP development currently at the disposal of local authorities is the Section 75 agreement (S106 in England). Local planning authorities are increasingly attaching Section 75/Section106 agreements to planning consent. However, there is enormous variation in the specifications and interpretation of these agreements with some requiring the developer simply to take all reasonable steps to implement a GCP, whilst others are required to develop a GCP with targets and obtain approval from the local authority before the planning consent is agreed. Furthermore, local authorities do not have sufficient information or knowledge about GCPs to use the Section 106 agreement effectively. There is insufficient evidence at the present time to indicate that a GCP of a given nature can produce a modal shift reduction of x percent, and therefore it is difficult to defend stringent GCP S106/S75 requirements at inquiry.

2.4.3 Image

A small number of GCPs have been implemented as a result of distinct company ethos and environmental values. In this way, organisations such as The Body Shop and RSPB have established GCPs to reflect their corporate environmental beliefs. Similarly, the associated image of a 'good' or 'conscientious' employer may encourage GCP development.

The motivation to address 'transportation' in many of the large national and multinational companies has emerged from their commitment to 'environmental responsibility'. Increasingly, organisations are starting to exert pressure on their suppliers to demonstrate 'green credentials', through ISO14001 or EMAS accreditation. This is a major motivation for many companies to start thinking about a GCP.

Enhancing public relations (PR) can also be an extremely important motivator for some organisations to design a GCP, although it is important to note that PR 'serves a purpose'. For example, a GCP is often one of a number of initiatives an organisation may involve itself with in an attempt to promote itself as the 'employer of choice' in a region, to assist with recruitment and retention.

2.4.4 Leading by example

Government and local authorities are under increasing pressure to lead by example to encourage other organisations to develop GCPs. For some companies the core business revolves around expanding the 'environmental market' and therefore it is in their commercial interest to lead by example to develop environmental products, or approaches.

GCP implementation in the UK has usually stimulated by one, or a combination of the main factors mentioned above.

2.5 GCP Measures

Within those organisations who have implemented a GCP a broad range of incentives and disincentives have been used to influence travel behaviour. Measures include, for example, provision for cycling, car sharing, promotion of public transport, telecommuting and teleworking, parking control and new terms and conditions of work (see Table 2.1).

Table 2.1: GCP Measures

Initiatives implemented in Green Transport Plans	
Mode	**Measure**
Walking	Improved lighting and walkways
	Crossings in/adjacent to site
Cycling	Changing/shower facilities
	Pool cycles
	Bicycle loan scheme
	Good, secure parking provision
	Discount purchases of cycles & equipment
Public Transport	Provision of PT information at workplace
	Access to Rail Planner
	Discounted season tickets
	Liaise with local operators to operate new services
Car share	Staff travel survey to identify potential sharers
	Priority parking spaces for car sharers
	Guaranteed ride home (taxi)
New conditions of Employment	Flexi-time
	Telecommuting/ working
	Company car initiatives (phased out/altered)

2.6 GCP development

To help conceptualise how GCPs evolve within an organisation it is useful to consider the development of a GCP with reference to a basic stages of change model. The model can be used to illustrate the process of changing travel behaviour at number of different levels. However, the stages of change are not necessarily sequential and it is possible to begin the GCP process at any stage of the model and progress at different speeds. Relapse can occur at any stage during the evolution process, as illustrated in Figure 2.1. It is also important to note that specific elements of a GCP may progress at different speeds to one another, depending on the significance of the barriers that need to be overcome before its implementation.

2.6.1 Pre-contemplation

At this stage organisations may only be vaguely aware of GCP, or have only a basic understanding and little idea about how to progress. A strong car culture and an absence of a motivator may provide little impetus to proceed. This is currently the stage of a majority of organisations in the UK.

2.6.2 Contemplation

The organisation becomes aware of the purpose and potential of a GCP. This is often prompted by a specific transport issue, such as parking problems or Section 75/Section 106 agreement, which encourages further investigation.

2.6.3 Preparation

An organisation may now devote resources to develop a GCP. A staff travel survey is carried out to ascertain mode splits, attitudes etc. Negotiations with local transport providers and local authorities may also be undertaken.

2.6.4 Action

At this stage an organisation starts to implement elements of their GCP, possibly through a number of smaller stages:
Basic- information provision, interest free loans, car share scheme;
Incentives - priority spaces, discounted or subsidised tickets, provision of showers and changing facilities, cash-out parking spaces;
Disincentives - changing parking policy, restructuring company car policy.
Most organisations with a GCP have implemented basic measures and some incentives. To date few have introduced significant disincentives.

2.6.5 Maintenance

Organisations will need to continue to monitor impacts and manage the evolutionary process of GCP implementation. This can be a time-consuming process and may require the allocation of a specific staff member to be given responsibility for the day-to-day running of the plan. A continuous programme of review and marketing is required to reflect changes in circumstances and behaviour.

2.6.6 Relapse

This can occur at any stage and may be as a result of a number of factors, such as organisational restructuring, the departure of key members of staff or the disappearance of the problem, which precipitated the plan's implementation.

Figure 2.1: Stages of Change Model

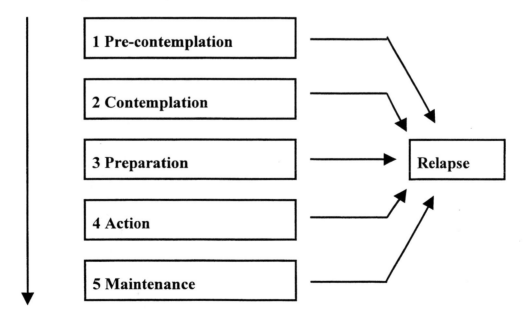

2.7 Conclusion

This Chapter has presented a brief summary of the history of and motivations for GCPs in the UK. It has also presented a model of their development which will assist in understanding why and how the two case studies in this research project are developing their GCPs in the manner described in the following two Chapters.

3. CHAPTER THREE

3.1 The Green Commuter Plan at Hewlett Packard

This section of the report summarises the progress which has been made by Hewlett Packard in implementing green commuting measures for its site at South Queensferry. By reviewing a number of different data sources this Chapter will explain the reasons for the development of the GCP, the reasons for the choice of measures which comprise it, the degree of involvement of different key actors in the plan implementation process, and the attitudinal reactions of a number of employees to their organisation's green commuting initiative. It will also show that the GCP at Hewlett Packard has changed employee modal split as intended. It will also present data to show the further effect that other GCP measures might have, were they to be implemented at HP.

The chapter is structured in the following way. Firstly it gives a description of the site, its location and accessibility by different modes of transport. It then considers current assistance provided by the company for employee transport. It goes on to present the results of HP's staff travel survey of November 1997 and discusses the impetus for and the elements of the green commuter plan (GCP) which emerged. It then considers the costs and benefits of the plan and any changes in government policy which might, in the opinion of those interviewed, make greening staff travel more straightforward. The report relies on a staff travel survey provided by HP and on the information and opinions given by the panel, and by the interviewees listed below.

The data used in this section are as follows. Firstly, in-depth interviews have been carried out with several key members of staff at Hewlett Packard (HP) South Queensferry. Staff to interview were selected on the recommendation of Ian McIntosh, Environmental Health and Safety Manager (EHSM), who has been the principal point of contact at HP for this work, and himself a key actor in the development of the GCP. Interviews lasted up to 90 minutes. The staff interviewed and the dates on which meetings took place are:

- Ian McIntosh, Environmental Health and Safety Manager, 28 October 1998
- Trevor Rae, Facilities Operations Manager (FOM), 22 October 1998
- Andy Belcher, Site General Manager (SGM), 2 February 1999
- Jim Stewart, Human Resources Manager (HRM), 5 March 1999
- Rosemary Scott, Compensation and Benefits Specialist (CBS), Human Resources Department, 5 March 1999

The second source of data is the travel survey and report on it which was carried out by HP in November 1997 to guide the development of its GCP. The third source of data is a questionnaire survey of a panel of employees who were also interviewed in March 1999 and who took part in focus groups in July and August 1999. Documents have been referred to, where these are available. A further section presents the results of the 1999 staff travel survey and compares these to the survey conducted in November 1997. The final data presented are from stated preference interviews with a random sample of 80 employees (stratified by mode) to discover their response to further, more interventionist, GCP measures that could be introduced at HP.

3.2 Description of HP / Agilent Technologies South Queensferry

HP is a multinational corporation with headquarters in Palo Alto, California. It manufactures electronics, computers, printers, telecommunication and control systems. The South Queensferry plant, founded in 1965, is divided into 3 divisions, all of which specialise in aspects of test equipment for telecommunications. They are the Telecomms Network Test Division (TNTD); Queensferry Microwave Division (QMD); and the Telecomms Systems Division (TSD). These operate relatively independently from one another, although functions key to green commuting, such as personnel (HR) and facilities management, are provided centrally. The Financial Services Centre for HP's entire UK operation is also sited at South Queensferry, as are the small Queensferry Solutions Centre and the sales operation for HP telecomms products for Scotland and northern England. An organisation chart is shown in Figure 3.1.

HP has been the subject of many studies of management and organisational behaviour, as it runs according to a management philosophy developed by its two American founders: this is "The HP Way". While the personal development of the individual employee lies at the heart of the HP Way, corporate social responsibility towards the global environment and the local community are also aspects of this corporate philosophy which are of direct relevance to green commuting. They are discussed in more detail later in the report.

On 1st November 1999 the HP Corporation embarked on a rationalisation of its businesses and decided to form two independent entities. The computing and peripherals operations, accounting for about 80% of the total turnover, was to retain the Hewlett-Packard title, whilst the new organisation, focusing on the manufacture of instrumentation and test equipment, was named Agilent Technologies. Agilent Technologies, Inc. (NYSE: A) is a global, diversified technology company focusing on high-growth markets in the communications, electronics, life sciences and healthcare industries. Agilent operates four businesses: test and measurement, semiconductor products, healthcare solutions and chemical analysis, supported by a central laboratory. Its businesses excel in applying measurement technologies to develop products that sense, analyze, display and communicate data.

Agilent's customers include many of the world's leading high-technology firms, which rely on Agilent's products and services to make them more profitable and competitive, from research and development through manufacturing, installation and maintenance. Agilent enables its customers to speed their time to market and to achieve volume production and high-quality, precision manufacturing.

Agilent's 42,000 employees and facilities located in more than 40 countries serve market-leading customers in over 120 countries. Major product development and manufacturing sites are located in the United States, China, Germany, Japan, Korea, Malaysia, Singapore, Australia and the United Kingdom. More than half of the company's net revenue is derived from outside the United States. The company's worldwide headquarters are in Palo Alto, California, in the heart of Silicon Valley.

3.3 General site details

The site is located in South Queensferry, a small free-standing town and ancient Royal Burgh of 5,000 people on the south shore of the Forth estuary immediately adjacent to the Forth Road and Rail Bridges. Administratively it is part of the City of Edinburgh. The 32 acre site houses five main buildings where some 1500 staff are based. While originally predominantly a manufacturing operation, the plant has developed into "higher value" activities such as R and D. An important part of this change occurred only two years ago (in 1996-7), when over 200 new, generally highly skilled, staff were hired.

A further change is now occurring: increases in operating targets and the location of a new Research and Development Division are bringing further increases in staff (40 over the past 6 months, with more to follow), and a new building is being constructed on one of the car parks. However, negotiations with City of Edinburgh Council and the landowner are on-going to construct 100 extra car parking bays on land immediately to the north of the site, with the current station car parking capacity increased to 147 spaces.

The site is immediately adjacent to Dalmeny station on the Fife Circle railway line, which provides 4 trains/hour each way (peak) and 3 trains/hour (off-peak) in each direction between Edinburgh and stations in east Fife; journey time to central Edinburgh is 11 - 15 minutes. Peak services in the peak direction (i.e. into Edinburgh in the morning and towards Fife in the evening) are full to capacity, but there are spare seats for those travelling in the non-peak direction. However, in the evening between 5.34 and 6.20 no train stops at Dalmeny in the Edinburgh direction. There are 2 buses an hour each way, to Edinburgh (east) and 1 per hour to Bo'ness (west). There are no direct bus links from the plant to either Fife to the north or other parts of West Lothian to the south-west although some buses from Fife do stop on the A90 at the south end of the Forth Road Bridge, and a Livingston bus is available at some points during the day.

Cycling conditions are generally good immediately around the site but trunk routes including the A90 Edinburgh-Fife road and A9000 to the west are congested and dangerous. The cycle path on the A90 is un-rideable on a road bike, although it is currently (February 2000) being upgraded. Outwith the peak, access by car is extremely good, but at peak times the Forth Road Bridge becomes heavily congested with commuters from Fife travelling to work in Edinburgh and West Lothian. (See Figure 3.2 for schematic map of site and access.) Some 985 parking spaces are provided; a new 80 space temporary car park was built in late 1997 to accommodate the cars of the growing workforce, but the long term aim is to manage without this facility. Other than visitors, spaces and those allocated to car poolers (see below), there are no reserved parking spaces for staff of any rank - all are on a first come first served basis. Current (Feb 2000) building work has reduced car parking availability by about 5% and there is now a significant overspill parking problem along Scotstoun Avenue, the western approach to the site, with consequent complaints from the local community. Park and ride activity at the station continues to grow with a severe parking problem on the site's northern approach road. With the site's increasing staff numbers, due to recent expansion, the company has again decided upon increasing car parking spaces for staff, while continuing to promote alternatives to single occupancy car use.

3.4 Hours of work

Normal work hours at the plant are 39 a week, worked on a flexitime schedule, with core hours of 0930-1600. However, about 70 employees work shifts at any one time. Trades Unions are not recognised and there are no unionised works councils or staff associations. The 'HP Way' encourages employee participation and representation is effective through the open door policy. Representative groups do exist, such as the Environment, Health and Safety Committee, to contribute to the formulation and review of site policies.

3.5 Company Transport

There are some 3 departmental pool cars and 57 employee company cars at the South Queensferry site. These 57 cars relate to the senior status of an employee as part of his/her remuneration package regardless of need. Some 159 staff are eligible for a company car but the majority (102) now opt to take a cash alternative, which is the monthly leasing cost for the car to which they would have been entitled, plus 32%. For the site HR manager this equates to about £530/month. The proportion taking the cash alternative has grown very rapidly, from about 50% in early 1998 to about 65% in early 1999. This is because very few of those eligible for perk cars do more than 2500 miles a year on business and so would have to pay tax at the highest rate on the perk. The cash alternative was introduced mainly because it is more fiscally advantageous for both company and employees; however, a subsidiary objective was to support HP's green commuting aims. As one respondent commented, *"If a benefit is changed as a cost containment measure, it can be marketed as a green measure as well."*

However, during 1999 a decision was made by site senior management to begin to phase out company cars for managers (there is a cash alternative scheme). Now all new leases on 'pool cars' are specified 'dual fuel' (Petrol/LPG). The first LPG van was on site during January 2000.

There is no allowance for cycling on works' business, nor interest-free loans available for season ticket purchase. Offers from external bodies regarding cycle discounts are advertised through the transport noticeboard. On works' trips, employees are encouraged to take the mode which maximises their productivity; as there is little local or regional travel, this mode is invariably the aeroplane.

Figure 3.1 – HP Organisational Chart

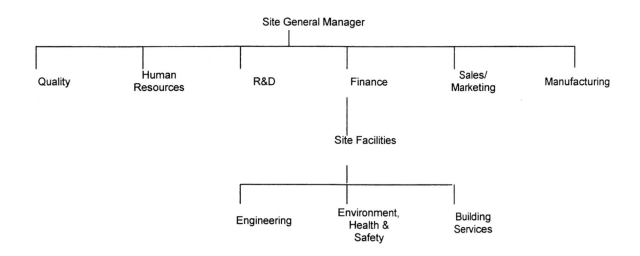

Note: There are 3 divisions: TSD, TNTD & QMD. Total of approximately 1,500 employees. Each division has roughly the same structure. IT reports to TNTD and similarly HR & Facilities report to TSD for convenience. This structure has not changed since HP became Agilent, apart from the addition of the new R+D division

Figure 3.2- HP Site Access Map

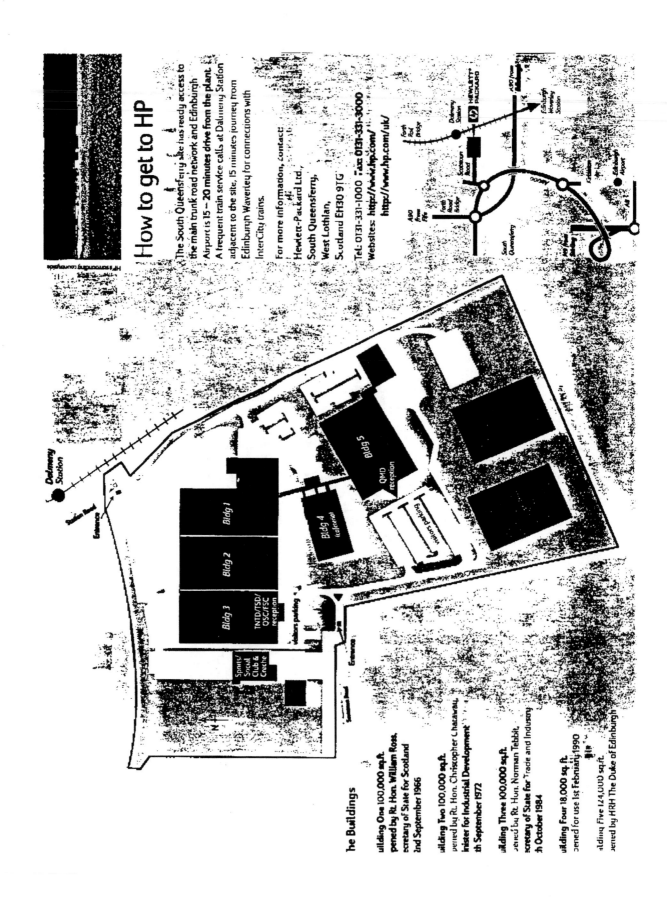

14

3.6 Motivations for HP's Green Commuter Plan

There are four main reasons for the emergence of green commuting at HP's South Queensferry site. These are:

1. To reduce pressure on parking.
2. To offer employees alternative and less stressful ways to commute other than the car.
3. Because of corporate environmental objectives.
4. Significant Environmental aspect. (ISO 14001 accredited site March 1995)

Different interviewees placed different levels of emphasis on these motivators: for the Facilities Department, parking was very important, while the Site General Manager cited environmental concerns as more significant. In its introduction, the report on the 1997 staff travel survey summarises these different motivations in the following statement:

> "Our site has experienced significant employee growth over the last few years and this trend will continue for some time. The car parking facilities on our site are now inadequate and the difficult decision to purchase a plot of land to provide additional spaces has now been taken to address current safety issues. HP cannot continue to support this growth in car parking facilities indefinitely. It is imperative that we analyse our employee needs and be ultimately able to ensure that suitable alternative transport is available to service the site. We also have a responsibility to reduce the impact on our environment and this strategy will help curb increases in atmospheric pollution which, together with a reduction in journey fatigue, can ultimately lead to a healthier workforce."

The majority of interviewees mentioned that the extra staff hired in 1996/97 caused additional pressure on car parking which focused minds on ways in which to reduce car commuting. Staff who arrived after 0900 began to encounter problems finding parking spaces; as one interviewee noted, *"there was a perception that the problem was becoming worse"*. This was a key impetus to the green commuting initiatives at HP.

In addition, the provision of a greater choice of modes, reducing stress and "setting the right tone" regarding employees' commuting habits all accord with HP's culture. Employees and management at HP accept that the company can and should advise staff on matters outwith the working environment, and this includes green commuting, but also other issues such as "work-life balance", advice on home security, and health promotion, both of which were mentioned in several interviews. The Facilities Manager felt that it was an important part of his role *"to create the right environment for people to do their best"*; he argued that if employees have a problems getting to their workplace or finding parking places when they get there, then their environment is sub-optimal.

Environmental management is an important part of HP's operations. The company has participated in the CBI's CONTOUR project on achieving excellence in Environmental Health and Safety, which highlighted the need to reduce the environmental impacts of employee transport. At the site level, the site general manager also argued that a desire to reduce the impact of commuting to HP on the local community was a further impetus to its GCP. Were parking pressures on site to become excessive, then overspill parking in local streets would be the undesirable result.

HP's Environmental Policy is set out in a booklet "Our Commitment to the Environment" contains a number of statements of relevance to green commuting. Firstly it notes that

"our goal is... to conduct our business worldwide in a responsible manner"

"excellence in environmental performance is consistent with our corporate objectives and essential to our continued business success"

"ensure that environmental policies, programs and performance standards are an integral part of our planning and decision-making process"

All these statements back up much of what was said by interviewees about HP's attempts to incorporate environmental responsibility into its production processes and to reduce its overall impact. However, a distinction was drawn by some between measures such as energy reduction or waste minimisation within the plant, which can directly save the organisation money, and green commuting, which has more disparate and less easily-quantified effects. This was expanded upon by the site general manager, who identified the company's key priorities as satisfying shareholders, customers and employees. Responsibility to the wider community comes after these first priorities - although it is still an important aspect of HP's activities world-wide. Other examples of HP South Queensferry's community participation include its work as part of the Edinburgh Lord Provost's Commission on Sustainable Development, its donation of PCs to local schools, and the active role it has played on the Chamber of Commerce Travel Planning Focus Group. (These activities have produced some publicity for HP's green commuting initiatives, which have given them added impetus.)

Finally, several interviewees mentioned that trips to other HP sites, particularly in the USA, had raised their awareness of green commuting issues and made them appear more acceptable in the South Queensferry context. As noted in "Our Commitment to the Environment":

"At many HP sites, we strive to reduce pollution from automobiles by offering our employees such services and programmes as telecommuting, discounts on transit passes, shuttles to and from train stations and our sites, and information on ride-sharing and other ways to commute".

In conclusion to this section, it is obvious that there have been many sources of impetus for HP's GCP, but that these relate to two main areas: environmental and corporate social responsibility; and "estate management" concerns regarding shortages of car parking and employee access to work.

3.7 1997 Staff Travel Survey

Once the decision was made by senior management and the Facilities Department that green commuting measures were appropriate at HP South Queensferry, the first step taken was to conduct a staff travel survey, so that existing patterns of and motivations for staff travel could be more fully understood. The survey would also provide a body of data which could then be used in negotiations with public transport providers for improved levels of service to the site.

This section provides a summary of the returns from the staff travel survey; for more details, the reader is referred to Appendix 3.2. The reader is also referred to the later section of this chapter that compares the 1997 travel survey with the 1999 survey. All staff (1,500 approx) at the site were surveyed and there was a 68% response rate – high for surveys of this type. Staff were asked about their current mode of transport to work, journey and start and finish times, distance travelled, and reasons for choice of current mode. They were also asked which mode they used as an alternative when their regular means of travel was out of action.

Some 64% of staff drive alone to work, but car-sharing was already quite popular, with almost 200 participating in carpools or lift-giving arrangements. In comparison, only about 100 staff regularly use public transport to get to work, and the vast majority of these use the train, as bus services are perceived as infrequent and unreliable. While approximately 75% of staff get to work in less than half an hour, the same proportion live 10 miles or more from work. The survey comments that, for those who live in areas which are not seriously affected by traffic congestion, it is difficult for any other mode of transport to offer this kind of door-to-door journey time over this distance. Main concentrations of staff home locations are in suburban Edinburgh and in south Fife (particularly Dalgety Bay, Dunfermline and Rosyth).

The survey revealed high levels of *occasional* rail use – some 200 staff as opposed to 50 regular users – and also found that the biggest deterrent to more regular use of the train was price, followed by frequency/reliability. It also found significant levels of occasional cycle use, but that the key deterrents to more regular use were the state of the A90 bike path and then the lack of secure parking and showers at work.

Given the high levels of occasional use of these two modes, and the existing high levels of car-sharing, it was decided to concentrate on these three areas as the core of the GCP: to improve the quality of cycle facilities on site and lobby for the A90 bike path upgrade; to set up a car-sharing scheme; and to negotiate with ScotRail for lower fares and hopefully better rail service to Dalmeny. The overall target for the GCP was set as a 10% reduction in employee car journeys to the site by 2000, with an interim target of a 5% reduction by the end of fiscal year 1998/99.

3.8 The measures that comprise the GCP

HP's Green Commuter Plan measures are as follows:

- Computerised car-pool matching with preferential parking for carpools with three or more occupants. There are currently 15 reserved spaces in locations close to building entrances.
- An informal emergency ride home service (only for true emergencies!)
- Improved bicycle parking (some are covered; all are monitored) and better shower facilities as part of an improvement to the on-site leisure centre. Cycle parking capacity has been doubled from about 40 to 80 spaces since the plan was adopted. The Site Facilities department is actively looking to improve cycling facilities, with drying room, overnight lockers and 'mini-changing areas' are planned for 2000/01.
- Negotiations with ScotRail for lower fares and better service to Dalmeny station. While only off-peak services have been improved (there are currently no spare trains at peak), the negotiations have resulted in a reduction of up to 40% in weekly season tickets prices for travel to Dalmeny. Prices are shown in Appendix 3.1.

- Negotiations with bus companies for improved service, and lobbying City of Edinburgh Council for an upgrade of the A90 bike path. As of March/April 1999, staff at HP were able to buy a discounted Lothian Region Transport (LRT) bus company annual season ticket (discount from the operator), but this will be of limited use as LRT no longer serves South Queensferry.
- Availability of public transport information on site, including access to Railtrack website. Also there is a newly constructed 'Site Transport Web-Page' for staff to use.
- Information provision on the green commuting initiatives via email, staff noticeboards, a regular transport update (see Appendix 3.1), and via the staff newspaper.
- An interest-free season ticket loan may be reviewed in the near future (administration logistics hinder this).

These measures took a matter of months to be implemented by the EHS manager, with the exception of the reduced rail fare, which took almost a year to negotiate. Procrastination does not appear to be part of the HP Way.

There were initial discussions, when developing the plan, about giving the benefit of the annual maintenance cost of a parking space (£200) to those who do not drive and therefore do not use a parking space. However, this was rejected by senior management on grounds of equity - only certain employees would receive it - and because of its cost and tax implications. One senior interviewee also expressed the opinion that free parking on site should not be seen as a staff benefit but more as an operational necessity.

There were also initial discussions about the possibility of charging staff to park on site, but this idea was also rejected because of fears of overspill into local streets. One interviewee felt that HP would not be prepared to be the first local company to try this option, as there would be likely to be significant negative reaction from at least some staff. However, several of those interviewed said that this position would be reviewed if the PNR parking levy was introduced in Edinburgh, as it would make the cost of employee parking a much more significant issue to the business.

At present there are no plans to extend the carpool parking to carpools with only two people in them. This is because it is believed that it would simply confer a privilege on many existing two-person carpools rather than leading to the formation of new ones.

The measures believed by interviewees to be the most effective are, firstly, the rail ticket discount; and secondly, the carpooling scheme (see also discussion of panel interviews, focus groups, SP survey and 1999 travel survey). No data on up-take of the former currently exists, but it was felt that cost of public transport was the biggest barrier to its further uptake and therefore that the discount was a very important measure. The carpooling scheme works well for those who are motivated in particular by the cost of commuting and for whom the disbenefit of greater inflexibility of travel times is outweighed by cost savings.

In late 1998 there did not appear to be a desire to implement other measures, at least until a second staff travel survey was conducted to measure how modal split has been affected by the existing measures. Several reasons were given for this relative stasis:

- It was seen to be extremely difficult to encourage further use of public transport to the site given that the service is not going to improve significantly until September 1999, when ScotRail anticipate an increase in the number of seats and the phasing out of "heritage" rolling stock.
- It was also difficult to actively encourage more staff to cycle, as to invite them to use the current A90 bike path is seen as tantamount to inviting them to risk their lives.
- There was a need to see how well the existing measures are working before adding to them.
- The tax status of green commuting benefits is a major disincentive to HP introducing financial incentives/disincentives for staff to change their commuting habits, the tax changes in the 1999 budget notwithstanding (these do not exempt subsidies for public transport use from personal taxation).
- Implicit in the interviews of senior staff was a reluctance to implement measures which required more resources (either monetary or in terms of staff time), or which introduced *disincentives* to commute by car, under current conditions. However, if government policy changes, HP's position may also change.

It could also be argued that the construction of the temporary car park and the stable number of employees at the site during 1998/99 eased the pressure on parking which existed in 1996-97 when recruitment was at a high level. However, these problems now appear to be returning.

3.9 Green Commuter Plan Marketing & Implementation

A site Environmental Management Council, composed of the three site General Managers, the Human Resources (HR) Manager, Facilities Manager and Environmental Health and Safety (EHS) Manager, meet regularly to set environmental priorities at the site level; it was this committee which provided direct management support to the green commuting initiatives and which gave those charged with their implementation direct access to senior management. A staff travel group composed of an HR specialist, the EHS manager and the Facilities manager meets more regularly to discuss progress and to agree further actions. As noted above, most of the measures took a relatively short time to implement.

The responsibility for the implementation of the majority of the measures rests with the EHS manager. The HR specialist is involved where measures have compensation and/or staff benefits implications. The most time-consuming task is the administration of the car-sharing scheme. Parking permits for the car pool parking bays are given to named car pool teams (of three or more). Hence only that team can park in a given space. This has given rise to some negative feedback when, for example, one member of a team is on holiday and so a team of only two appears to be parking in a reserved space, or when cars are absent, yet the space cannot be used by another. While dealing with such gripes absorbs a certain amount of time, the EHS manager said that the actual administration of the permits themselves is a straightforward task. A problem can arise when one or more team members move job and building within HP and the allocated parking space is no longer convenient for them. There is no waiting list at the current time (spring 1999).

The GCP is marketed and communicated within HP in a number of ways.

- A bi-monthly Transport Update is circulated by email and posted on noticeboards to let staff know about latest developments in green commuting.
- Coffee talks are held quarterly in each Division. These are an opportunity for staff to ask managers questions about all aspects of HP practice; green commuting has occasionally been a topic for discussion.
- There are periodic promotions using specific publicity to raise awareness of certain elements of the GCP - e.g. a "launch" of the upgraded cycle parking.
- Email is used more generally, for example to market the car-sharing scheme.
- There is a generally open environment and a current philosophy of "management by wandering around" which allow anyone who has a query about commuting to easily approach the appropriate member of staff to answer their query.
- Intranet site giving information about the plan and its history, and providing relevant links (an extract is provided in Appendix 3.1).

There is no doubt that communication has been a key part of the HP plan.

3.10 Benefits and Costs

The benefits and costs of the GCP at HP have not been quantified. Interviewees explained that the main costs - the EHS Manager's time, and the costs of additional cycle parking and carpool parking bays - were absorbed into an existing budget and that for this reason there was little reason to monitor them precisely. Management was willing for some resource to be committed to a project which they perceived to be broadly beneficial, without requiring a full business case to be made. Appraisal could, it was pointed out, require more resources to carry out than its results would justify. However, several interviewees also noted that a full business case *would* be required if more resources were put into the plan: if, for example, bus fares were subsidised or a full-time member of staff had to be hired to administer the GCP. This final point does represent a barrier in making a business case to justify the planning of a potentially more effective GCP.

The obvious main financial saving for HP from the GCP is the reduction in requirement for on-site parking and its maintenance. The Facilities department quotes a capital cost of £2000/space and an annual maintenance figure of £200. However, one senior interviewee felt that this was not a cost which the company would necessarily take into account: whether or not the land was used for car parking, there would be an attached maintenance cost, while the capital cost of a space annualised over 20 years was judged by him to be insignificant in comparison to many other costs. In his view, the cost of parking would become a serious issue for the business only when there were significant opportunity costs attached to it, or when HP simply runs out of room for more parking on-site. At present (February 2000), however, it is negotiating to expand its parking.

3.11 Attitudes to Green Commuting at HP

A very strong message was conveyed by all those interviewed that there was in principle support for GCP activities at HP and that it is very much in tune with existing practices, environmental management and corporate social responsibility. Examples of clear management support were provided. These were:

- The time given by management to the planning of initial GCP measures.
- The covering letter from the Site Manager sent out with the staff travel survey.
- Time contributed by senior managers to this research project.

However, it was pointed out by one respondent that many managers do retain their company cars and thus, implicitly at least, can be seen to be giving support to "non-green" commuting. In contrast, few "lead by example" in their choice of mode of transport to work (although the Site General Manager has cycled to work on a few occasions). Most of those interviewed did feel, however, that it is impractical for the most senior managers to use alternative modes due to their very irregular working hours and constant travel on business.

There were interesting parallels drawn between company health campaigns and green commuting. Both are attempting to encourage changes in attitudes and lifestyle which fit in with HP's corporate philosophy and which provide benefits to employer and employee - but benefits which may be difficult to quantify. One key interviewee was of the opinion that the benefits of health campaigns were much easier to identify than those of green commuting, and that there were fewer potential drawbacks to the former. He was particularly concerned that the encouragement of green commuting should not negatively affect employees by lengthening their journeys to work or reducing the quality of their commute; he felt strongly that alternative modes should offer at least as good a "commute experience" as the car if green commuting was to be something which managers would be very keen to recommend to their staff. However, the current quality of public transport in particular gives him reason to doubt that it can offer the quality of commute which he thinks is required.

3.12 Corporate culture at HP and its influence on the development of the Green Commuter Plan

Research in travel demand management suggests that corporate culture is amongst the variables which can aid or hinder the implementation of a GCP. For example, the effective dissemination of information, which is critical to the successful implementation of GCPs (Rye, 1997), can be hindered if there are many layers of hierarchy in the organisation. The commitment of senior management to a GCP programme can be important if the culture is such that the workforce is used to reacting mainly to direction from the top. The frequency of change management programmes can lead to a rejection of new practices which are not compulsory. Inclusion of senior management in the discussions leading to the introduction of a GCP, particularly when coupled with commitment to "lead by example" in the GCP, can influence the behaviour of others in their travel patterns.

It is accepted that the internal structure of an organisation contributes to explaining and predicting behaviour of employees within it (Robbins, 1998; Mullins, 1998). The basis of this argument hinges on the idea that organisational structure reduces ambiguity for employees, clarifies concerns over what and how work is processed and by thus shaping attitudes, facilitates greater motivation and higher performance levels.

It is also the case that the structure of the organization imposes constraints on employees in that it limits and controls what they do. In general, organisations structured around high levels of formalisation and specialisation, with strict adherence to a chain of command, incorporating limited delegation of authority and narrow spans of control, will give employees little autonomy.

Hewlett Packard, at the Queensferry plant, use a model incorporating low formalisation, and wide spans of control and delegation of authority. Shared plans are developed for achievement of the work objectives and the company applies the principle of open communication. This is operationalised in practices such as valuing different perspectives, making use of informal communication networks, and having open plan offices and open doors. The company workforce has flexibility in their hours of attendance at the workplace. This model provides employees with greater autonomy and it is usual to see this characterised by greater behavioural diversity (Luthans, 1997). An organisation chart is shown in Figure 3.1 on page 11.

The culture of an organisation refers to the system of shared meaning held by employees, which distinguish the organisation from others. This can be seen another way as the key characteristics valued by the organisation (Becker, 1982; Schein, 1985). HP adopts a people- and team-orientation approach as reflected in their five underlying organisational values which are:

1. We have trust in and respect for individuals
2. We focus on a high level of achievement and contribution
3. We conduct our business with uncompromising integrity
4. We achieve our common objectives through teamwork
5. We encourage flexibility and innovation

(From *"Communicating the HP Way"*, 1989)

Research suggests that in a strong culture these core values will be widely accepted and the greater the commitment of the workforce to these values, the stronger the culture. In turn, a strong culture will have a great influence on the behaviour of the members of the organisation as the high degree of sharing and intensity creates a climate of behavioural control. Within HP there is a clear agreement over what the organisation stands for, which has built cohesiveness, loyalty and commitment to the organisation. In short, there is undoubtedly a strong culture. Indications are that, given the hierarchical strong culture approach used at HP, there is likely to be a high level of support for the introduction of a GCP.

3.13 Panel survey

A panel of 57 HP staff was selected to enhance the quality of behavioural and attitudinal data gathered at this case study site. The purpose of this was to provide time-series data over the length of the project to give a more complete picture of the way in which attitudes to and travel behaviour change as a result of the GCP. It should be stressed that the panel were volunteers and hence self-selected, rather than a random sample of HP staff. However, as the following data reveal, they are representative of the workforce as a whole in terms of their mode choice for commuting (see Table 3.4: although the number of rail users in the panel may appear to be over-represented, this may be accounted for by the small sample size).

The panel members have been surveyed with a more in-depth travel questionnaire than that used in the 1997 staff travel survey; nonetheless, where possible, comparisons have been made. The purpose of this was to provide in-depth information to form the basis of interviews with panel members. These took place during March 1999 to probe their attitudes to (green) commuting in greater depth. The results presented here are those from the 1999 panel survey, interviews and focus groups, the schedules for which can be found in Appendix 3.3.

3.13.1 Characteristics of the HP Panel Members

There were 49 survey forms returned, a response rate of 86%. Some 80% of the panel were aged between 25 and 44, and 82% were male. Twenty respondents live in households with children – this can be an important factor in mode choice for the trip to work, as children often have to be dropped off on the way. While certain members of the panel live as far away as Glasgow, North Lanarkshire and the Borders, 36 live 8 miles or less from work, and the average travel distance to work is 10.4 miles (7.8 if the extreme outliers are removed).

3.13.2 Car ownership and travel to work

All 49 respondents have a current driving licence and 46 have access to a car. Of the 3 respondents who do not have access to a car, 2 travel by train and 1 travels to work as part of a car share agreement. The respondents were asked to identify their usual means of transport to work and the responses are summarised in Table 3.1.

Table 3.1: Mode for travel to work.			
	Panel		1997 Survey
Mode of travel	Number	%	%
Car (not sharing)	29	59	65
Car share	10	20	20
Train	5	10	5
Train/walk	3		
Cycle/train	1	10	10
Cycle	1		
All modes	49	100	100

Respondents were asked to estimate the weekly cost of their travel and these are set out in Table 3.2. The average cost for the 10 respondents who do not use a car is less than half of the cost estimated by those who car commute alone. There is some evidence that the cost of car sharing is seen to increase progressively as the number of sharers increases. One reason for this may be that longer commuting distances – up to 40 miles in some cases - tend to be associated with more passengers and that these distances do involve relatively higher costs per person. (Note: because of the small sample size it is not possible to be definitive about this).

Table 3.2: Average travel cost/week for staff by mode of travel and number of sharers.				
Mode of travel	Number who share	Respondent total	Average weekly cost(£)	Average travel Distance (miles)
Cycle	-	1	6.00	7
Cycle/train	-	1	7.00	7
Train	-	5	12.36	7.4
Train/walk	-	3	14.03	7.6
Car (not sharing)	-	29	26.39	9.6
Car share	1	5	10.80	9.4
Car share	2	2	11.00	7.5
Car share	3	3	13.67	32

An important issue in green commuter surveys is the alternative mode used by commuters when, for some reason, their normal mode of transport is out of action, as this gives an indication of how easy (or not) it may be to encourage them to use this alternative more frequently. Interestingly, of the 7 respondents who do not car commute 4 will use a car if their usual mode is not available. In contrast, public transport is favoured by 14 of the 21 non car-sharing commuters, while the remaining 6 would car share. Again public transport is favoured as an alternative by 6 of the 7 respondents who currently car share their journey to work.

3.13.3 Factors which influence choice of mode

The respondents were asked to rate the importance of travel factors that influenced their choice of mode on a scale of 1 to 7, where 1 is not important and 7 is most important. Thus any factor scoring more than 3.5 is more than averagely important. The results are tabulated in Table 3.3. The average values for the factors require careful interpretation because they do not necessarily represent the "performance" of the factor but rather the view of its influence in mode choice.

Non car commuters appear to be more influenced by shorter journey times than car commuters, while other factors have more influence with car commuters. Interpretation of the responses to factor (b) does not necessarily imply that commuting without a car is less reliable but rather that people who do so may be prepared to accept less reliability.

Table 3.3: Average strength of interest of travel factors by car commute.			
Factor influencing mode choice for journey to work	Commute by car?	Count of responses	Average of response[2]
(a) This is the shortest travel time for home-work journey.	No	8	5.38
	Yes	38	5.21
(b) This is the most reliable mode.	No	7	4.57
	Yes	36	5.19
(c) Cost of this mode is lower than via an alternative mode.	No	9	4.00
	Yes	37	4.05
(d) This mode allows for non-work related stops to be Made en-route.	No	7	3.00
	Yes	37	4.19
(e) Irregular working hours are a feature of my position.	No	7	4.43
	Yes	37	4.51
(f) This mode is the safest form of travel to/from work.	No	7	4.00
	Yes	36	2.36
(g) There is a walk exceeding 10 mins from my Home to the nearest bus/rail halt.	No	7	2.14
	Yes	32	3.03

Many respondents expanded on these factors with comments, explaining the specifics of their journeys to work and (in the case of car drivers) the lack, for their personal trip, of an alternative that they perceived to be viable. The flexibility of the car was also important. For public transport users, reduced stress on the journey to work was an important factor, whilst cyclists mentioned the benefit of being able to keep fit on the way to work. A full list of comments is provided in Appendix 3.4.

3.13.4 Access to pool cars

Respondents were asked about the availability of pool cars, as the need for a car for works business is frequently cited in such surveys as a reason to drive to work. Only 4 respondents indicated that they required their car for work purposes during the day. Of these 4, all stated that a pool car was also available. This is because the majority of perk car holders at HP make their car available for pool use during the day in order to be able to claim the free petrol allowance. It is not known if the pool was used or not. A scheme like this is not unique although it may be unusual – some local authorities, for example, require cars leased to specific individuals (for work and private use) to be used as pool cars when required.

---

[2] Responses ranged from 1 = least influence to 7 = greatest influence

3.13.5 Working hours and potential for working from home

The vast majority (43) of respondents have flexible working hours. Core times differ quite significantly and the actual times worked too show a range of start and finish times. Over half (30) of the respondents also indicated that overtime was a regular feature of their work. There was, however, no consistent pattern to this, with some respondents indicating they work some overtime most days whilst with others it was an end-of-the-month feature. Only 1 (one) respondent works part-time and only 1 (one) has a shift work pattern.

Telecommuting has significant potential to increase productivity while reducing commuting travel. Of the 49 panel respondents, 28 stated it would be possible to work from home and of these, 71% (20) believed there was scope to increase their hours. The average number of days being worked at home is greater among those respondents who feel they could do more than they do at present. The reasons stated (where provided – 7 gave no reason) fell into two main categories: the first was work-related, in that the respondent's job requires them to be available to meet face to face with colleagues; and the second was family-related, in that respondents felt that working at home in the presence of demanding children would not be feasible.

3.13.6 Additional measures in the Green Commuter Plan

Appendix 3.4 lists the measures that the 28 respondents who provided this information feel should be in a Green Commuter Plan. Whilst there is no major theme to the responses, there is an emphasis on improvements that can be made to public transport services particularly in relation to cost, ticketing, improved frequency and information. Several respondents are also aware of more complex issues such as the variable versus fixed costs of motoring and the tax status of company-provided travel benefits. Cyclists are keen to see safer routes, particularly to and from Edinburgh. Importantly for car-drivers the majority of the measures which they cite as influencing their choice of mode relate to the quality and cost of public transport. This has been examined further by the use of stated preference (SP) techniques (see below). From the point of view of the commuter planner at HP, there is relatively little that the organisation itself can do to improve these aspects of the commute, other than provide direct subsidy, or lobby public transport operators.

3.13.7 Measures introduced to encourage greener commuting: involvement and effect

Of the 49 respondents, only 1 (one) stated that he/she had been involved in discussions regarding the promotion of a Green Commuter Plan (there was one "no response"). Table 3.4 shows what influence these measures have personally on the respondents. The measure with the biggest effect was the reduction in the rail fares to and from Dalmeny, with those employees who do not commute by a car giving it an average score of over 6. Even although it had the highest effect for car commuters, the score they gave was less than 3. Other public transport and cycle related measures were also much more highly scored by non-car commuters. The introduction of dedicated car parking spaces for car sharing groups was not highly scored by either group. This information has significant implications for the GCP at HP, since those whose modal choice it is attempting to influence do not appear to rate its components very highly. This finding is supported by the full 1999 travel survey; however, the SP experiment indicates that more interventionist measures such as direct financial incentives and disincentives to change mode would have a much greater effect on those who currently (March 2000) drive alone to work.

Table 3.4: Average response to GCP measures (scored out of 7)	Commute by car?	Count	Average response[3]
(a) Introduction of dedicated car parking spaces for car sharing groups.	No	10	1.10
	Yes	38	1.63
(b) Provision of increased cycle stands and associated facilities.	No	10	2.80
	Yes	39	1.36
(c) The reduction in rail fares to and from Dalmeny.	No	10	6.20
	Yes	37	2.86
(d) Provision of information on rail/bus travel via notice boards.	No	10	2.90
	Yes	3	1.89
(e) Provision of information on rail/ bus travel via e-mail.	No	10	3.10
	Yes	38	2.13

Six respondents have indicated that they changed mode as a result of the introduction of these measures. Table 3.5 details whether or not this change has been maintained.

Table 3.14: Reasons for changing mode		
Mode of travel	Details of change	Maintained up to March 1999
Car (not sharing)	Tried use of train for a period.	No
Train	Reduction of rail fares to and from Dalmeny.	Yes
Cycle/train	Started to move away from the car before HP changed.	Yes
Train/walk	I switched from the bus to the train when fares went down.	Yes
Car (not sharing)	Cycling more.	Yes
Train/walk	Due to reduction in rail fare, it is now economical to take the train and not drive.	Yes

3.14 Panel Interviews

Following the self-completion questionnaires completed by the panel in January 1999, in-depth interviews which took place during March and April. All bar two panel members were interviewed. The purpose of the interviews was to expand on the themes which had been explored in the questionnaire survey and in particular to explore the motivations and reasoning behind particular attitudes and behaviour.

The summary of key findings and detailed findings should be read in conjunction with the Questionnaire, Focus Group and Interview Schedules in Appendix 3.3. This schedule formed the structure of each interview but, where appropriate, interviewers departed from it to probe certain issues in more depth or to gain a greater appreciation of certain motivations or attitudes. Interviews took place on site at Hewlett Packard and each lasted approximately 30 minutes.

---

[3] Responses ranged from 1 = little effect to 7 = much effect

3.15 Findings: Individual Behaviour

The first section of the interview schedule dealt with panel members' individual behaviour and the motives underlying this. It also briefly covered their views on the necessity for HP to encourage green commuting.

3.15.1 Choice of mode

The first question considered the issue of the reason for people's choice of mode. It was notable that many of the panel had in fact considered public transport and, in many cases, used it when their home life circumstances had been different. However, for those who are now car users, cost is not the major factor influencing their mode choice. Instead, they use the car because of its flexibility, and because it can be the only reasonable option, given childcare responsibilities and/or home location. Many believe that they do not live close enough to the nearest railway station for the train to offer a journey time competitive to the car. For most, congestion on the Forth Bridge is not a sufficient deterrent, particularly since many are commuting at the shoulders of the peak. A particularly detailed explanation of mode choice was made by the following commuter, who now drives alone to work:

> "I used to car share and also take the train from Rosyth. I moved house to Dunfermline and walked to the station and took the train. I moved house again and its not realistically possible to take a bus and train. There is a long walk from the nearest bus stop for buses to the station. So I went back to using the car. I have tried where I could to use public transport - if I lived in Germany I would. I would change back to the train if there was a close train station or the bus goes to the station."

Another put it more succinctly:

> "I'm used to irregular and unpredictable working hours and the car gives me convenience."

Amongst those who use alternatives to driving alone, there were two employees who had switched to the train in response to the reduction in season ticket prices. All those who actually travel by train do so because for them it offers a reduced level of stress together with a comparable journey time to that by car. However, there is some disquiet that there is a large gap in northbound services from Dalmeny between 17.30 and 18.30, which is inconvenient for many people. Through continued discussion with Scotrail, the times have been amended slightly to reduce this gap. As of May 28th 2000 the new time will allow only a 38 minute interval. It is instructive that none of the panel uses the bus, and all appeared to view the train as the only potentially viable form of public transport to the site.

Of those panel members who car share, most do so to reduce both their commute costs and the stress of their trip to work. The average distance travelled to work by car sharers 14.6 miles) is greater than by those who drive alone (12.2 miles)[4]. This finding replicates those of many earlier studies: in general, at longer travel to work distances, the inconvenience of car-sharing

---

[4] Source: Hewlett Packard Travel Survey 1997.

begins to be outweighed by the advantages of reduced cost and stress. As one car sharer noted:

"For two and a half years I've car pooled from Glasgow. Four's a good number - the advantage is that it's a long drive and we're only required to drive in turn."

However, a few members of the panel cited either environmental or health reasons for their choice of (alternative) mode. This was the case for a keen cyclist who travels from south west Edinburgh; and for one of the car sharing members of the panel, who commutes only a relatively short distance, from Dunfermline.

3.15.2 Propensity to change mode

In general those panel members who drive alone report that a big change would be required before they would use a different mode. This might be a change in the home circumstances or location which currently constrains their mode choice, or, from the supply side, there would have to be very significant improvements to public transport timings, reliability, comfort, cost, frequency and routes. This reflects the findings of the earlier questionnaire survey. One panel member reflected the views of many others when he said:

"Where I live the first bus leaves at 07.25 and I would have to walk to the plant from the end of the Forth Road Bridge. The bus therefore is not an option. I would Park and Ride from Cowdenbeath but there is no secure parking there. I could also Park and Ride from Dalgety Bay but once you've driven that far you might as well carry on. I have car shared in the past and was asked to do it again, but I declined because of times, and the lack of flexibility."

While there were some panel respondents who made comments such as:

"there is nothing HP could do to encourage me to change mode, because of my personal circumstances",

about half of those who drive alone do believe that HP could do more to encourage a change of mode. Suggestions included shuttle buses across the Bridge, subsidies for public transport fares, and (further) improvements to facilities for cyclists. Others suggested that HP could do more lobbying work with public transport providers to improve services to the site. The majority of those who already use alternative modes believe that HP could do more to support them with further improvements to public transport services. It should be borne in mind, however, that the panel questionnaire showed clearly that those who currently drive alone do not feel that the current range of green commuting incentives offered by HP has a significant influence on their choice of mode.

3.15.3 The role of HP in encouraging Green Commuting

There was an all-round resounding **yes** that HP should – as a large company – have a responsibility to take an interest into how its employees get to work and seek to influence choice of mode. There were one or two dissenters from this line who felt that

"it's the individual's responsibility"

29

but the majority supported the principle of HP's green commuting initiatives because of

- its commitment to corporate social responsibility. As one respondent said, *"One of its five principles is citizenship."*
- its commitment to the environment. *"We should be interested in the environment and what we're doing to it. HP should take an active role to encourage staff to use cars less."*
- the need to resolve or mitigate on-site and local congestion and parking problems. It was of note that this more business-orientated line was not solely confined to the solo car drivers: one cyclist commented that HP should only get involved in these activities *"if a direct business need or advantage were to result. Staff are rewarded on profit and anything that takes profit affects pay."*

There was a strong feeling from staff and managers that, while green commuting should be encouraged, this encouragement should be low key and informal.

> *"I would encourage them to do what they feel comfortable with to get best performance. No pressure to change. I'd make people aware of options by being proactive but short of active encouragement - it's not the HP Way."*

This view was justified by most on the grounds that, while the company has some responsibility to be a good corporate citizen, commuting is an issue which strays into the realm of home life and is therefore ultimately a personal choice:

> *"I have a role in informing but not directing individual travel patterns"*

was a typical comment.

3.15.4 Travel costs

The panel interviews gave the opportunity to probe perceptions of travel costs in greater detail. By and large travel costs of current mode and alternatives are not well researched. Even where panel members have stated that quoted costs were fully calculated, this still requires to be treated with caution. Most panel members take into account only the variable costs of car use and therefore underestimate the full cost of driving to work. Car drivers in particular were very uncertain about the cost of taking public transport to work but, as many of them pointed out, this was because for most of them time and convenience were key determinants of mode choice, not cost.

3.15.5 Parking

Respondents were asked whether they perceived HP's provision of parking spaces for its employees as a subsidy to car drivers. This notion was almost universally *not* supported. A common theme was – *it would be a subsidy in town but not on a green field site.* This echoes the findings of other studies (eg Rye, 1997). Parking was seen either as a measure which the company should provide to assist its employees who choose to drive in the same way as cycle parking or a safe route to the station helps those who choose to cycle or take the train. A further recurring theme was that free parking at work was a recruitment/retention tool.

3.15.6 Telecommuting

Panel members were given more opportunity to expand on the ideas they had commented on in the questionnaire about telecommuting. There was a positive and realistic view of both its benefits and its constraints. Some panel members already telecommute some of the time, others were very keen to try it, but some recognised that the nature of their job made it impossible to work from home. Panel members reported that HP culture and management are favourably disposed to this form of working where it makes sense, and where work is based on outputs rather than the member of staff's actual presence.

3.16 Findings: organisational issues

The second section of the interview discussed panel members' perceptions of the importance of green commuting within HP and the motivations for its implementation. Issues including the communication of the GCP message, and the role of management in encouraging their staff to consider greener modes of transport, were also discussed here.

3.16.1 Does HP have a transport problem?

There was a resounding "yes" in answer to this question. Car drivers perceived slightly less of a problem than did users of other modes, but in general there was a view that parking, the speed of cars along the western access to the plant, Scotstoun Avenue, and lateness caused by problems on the Forth Road Bridge, were all concerns for the company and therefore one of the main reasons for the adoption of the GCP. One respondent encapsulated these problems succinctly when they said:

> "Yes, there is a problem. There's parking off-site; the speed of cars on Scotstoun Avenue; the price of public transport; and if there is an accident on the Forth Road Bridge then there are delays and people are late into work through no fault of their own."

But these were not perceived to be major problems - as one panel member commented,

> "The big caveat is that extra space for car parking might be better used for output, but attention to and time spent on travel patterns tends to be low on the priority list... It's something the General Managers are interested in under Any Other Business".

3.16.2 Communication of Green Commuting issues

This perception was very much reiterated when discussion moved on to the communication of green commuting issues by managers and staff. Whilst panel members had some awareness of green commuting issues, and some claimed to discuss commuting in general with their colleagues - in the context of congestion on the bridge, for example - they were only able to report very occasional, ad hoc, feedback of information by managers. Managers simply do not appear to care about how staff get to work, as long as they get there on time and able to work. Panel members did remember receiving emails from the Facilities Department, this appeared to be the full extent of their awareness. Two typical comments were:

"There is no discussion about green commuting but people complain about traffic on their way to work."

"Staff do not discuss green commuting. But if you come in by train, you get a funny look. In general there is very little communication about green commuting."

It was commented that green commuting is not part of HP's top-down management policy, but rather an add-on which merits only an occasional mention at staff chats, for example. The feeling that it was not a management priority came up time and again:

"I would actively mention it but only if part of higher management communication... It's not high on the list of priorities and there's no requirement by managers to raise the issue."

By way of comparison, staff were asked about management encouragement to use the gym, and for staff to strive for a sensible work-life balance. In earlier interviews with senior management, both of these had been flagged up as initiatives with parallels to green commuting. In the panel discussions, use of the gym was seen as very much a personal decision, but there was a perception of much more active management support for work-life balance. This was presumably because it was an issue which was accorded high priority by senior management because of the links between work-life balance and employee productivity. The following comments was typical:

"Yes I do. I always recommend a work-life balance (it's the HP thing). Green commuting is not a part of it."

Green commuting at HP has some way to go before it achieves this level of awareness, acceptance and management support. There is a role for the proponents of the GTP in stressing the benefits of green commuting and any possible links between it and work-life balance.

3.16.3 Car parking and green commuting

Echoing the view of parking as an operational necessity, car drivers (non-sharing) overwhelmingly felt that HP should not charge for parking to subsidise other modes. The feeling on this issue was more mixed for other groups of commuters. Views were mixed on charging for parking in the future, but there was a feeling that external pressures, particularly government, may force the issue. Some panel members also recognised that the land currently used for parking had an opportunity cost attached and that it might in future be needed for additional buildings, in which case there would be more justification for charging for car parking.

3.17 Panel Focus Groups

Two focus groups with panel members were carried out at HP on consecutive days. A schedule is set out in Appendix 3.3. These revealed a number of important perceptions of HP's GCP and of the ways in which it could be made more effective. The groups were held as follows:

Date	Time	Number in Group
1 July 1999	14.00-15.00	8
2 July 1999	11.00-12.00	10

Firstly, the groups revealed some lack of awareness about the car-sharing scheme in spite of what its organisers had thought was relatively saturation publicity. However, it is important to note that emails, one of the principal methods of information distribution in the organisation, are sent to line managers who can then decide, or not, to pass the message on to their employees. There was a clear perception that these managers could at times be a significant barrier to information dissemination. There was also a feeling that the cycling facilities, though improved, still did not offer any reasonable clothes storage and were not distributed widely enough around the buildings on the site to be convenient.

The groups were very clear that the primary motivation for the company to pursue a GCP at this site was to manage demand for parking and to reduce the dangers associated with traffic circulating in the car park. Most participants felt that there was a clear link between the GCP and HP's commitment to "Good Corporate Citizenship", but that this was very much a secondary motivation which nicely complements the first.

It was difficult for focus group participants to come to any conclusions about the level of organisational importance currently attributed to the GCP compared to when it first started. If anything, a small majority felt that it was less of an organisational priority now than it has been, but that this is something which very much ebbs and flows.

3.17.1 Likely further measures to be implemented at HP

Section 3.6 gave details of interviews with managers at HP from whom a strong message emerged that it was unlikely that this site would implement any more contentious or expensive measures, because there is currently no clear business case for so doing. If problems became more acute, or a PNR parking levy introduced, then this would be likely to lead to the implementation of stronger but more resource-hungry GCP measures. Thus at the current time there is no indication that the GCP will broaden, although it may be promoted afresh and subject to some review after the results of the next travel survey are known.

The focus group respondents were asked to brainstorm on additional measures which they felt that HP could implement in order to increase the number of people using alternative modes to work. There was a minority of participants who felt that the current alternatives are so poor that there was nothing that the company could do to encourage people to use it. As one said, *"The chance of being caught in a traffic jam is less than being delayed by a train"* and, another, *"If they gave the train for free I wouldn't use it"*.

However, a much larger group of participants felt that it was crucial for the company to increase its lobbying of rail operators and the government to encourage them to improve services. This lobbying function was seen as an acceptable and effective activity, more so than the company itself paying for additional public transport services – although one participant suggested that the company could *"bung ScotRail a few quid"*.

33

Participants came up with many suggestions for further GCP measures. Many of these have been implemented in GCPs elsewhere and it is perhaps testimony to the HP panel's insight into the subject that they were able to develop these ideas. They were asked to rank possible measures in order of their potential effect on modal split, and also to consider how likely the company would be to implement each of them. Likelihood of implementation was seen to be related both to the cost of the measure to the company and its potential contentiousness among staff. There was also a recognition that if external conditions changed – in particular if a parking levy were introduced by government – then measures would be much more likely to be implemented.

It is also notable that certain measures, such as improved public transport information, have already been implemented as part of the HP GCP but there is a perception among the panel that there is a need for further improvement – by, for example, putting public transport information on the intranet. In the following table, effectiveness and likelihood of implementation of potential measures are categorised as high, moderate or low (H, M or L).

Table 3.5: Potential further GTP measures

Measure	Effectiveness	Likelihood of implementation
Lobbying service providers	H	H
Better cycle facilities	M	M
On-site facilities (e.g. creche)	M	M
Telecommuting	H	M
Compressed work week	H	L
Employee transportation co-ordinator	H	L
Shoe incentive	L	L
Parking spaces for 2+ carpools	M	M
Financial incentive to use green mode	H	L
Better public transport information	L	H
Parking charges	M	L

It can be seen that those measures perceived to be the most effective are often also those thought to be less likely to be implemented. There was considerable opposition to parking charges on the grounds that they would be inequitable and would also be likely to simply shift the problem to surrounding residential streets, thus undermining HP's desire to be a good corporate citizen.

3.18 Stated Preference Study

Napier TRI's proposal for this study undertook to carry out stated preference interviews with a sample of HP staff in order to understand and to able to predict their responses to potential GCP measures, as it was recognised that there were some potentially very powerful measures (such as charged parking, or subsidies provided by HP, to those employees using public transport) that were unlikely to be implemented but whose effects should in any case be explored.

From the responses to the 1999 travel survey (see below), a random sample of 80 employees was drawn, stratified by the range of modes used by HP staff. In collaboration with the client, an SP survey instrument was designed and piloted. It was then administered, by a Napier researcher, in individual interviews of, on average, 30 minute duration; these took place during

January 2000. The survey instrument was designed to elicit from respondents their modal choice, given a variety of different scenarios for packages of measures in any future GCP. Typically, respondents would be asked to trade off travel time by one mode against travel time by another, or cost and parking search time, or an incentive to use a green mode against travel time by car. Only relevant questions were asked to respondents: for example, existing carsharers were not asked about incentives to make them carshare. The results are presented below; the survey instrument is illustrated in Appendix 3.5.

3.18.1 Stated preference results

These results should be read in conjunction with the survey instrument; however, essentially, respondents were presented with different scenarios featuring packages of incentives and sometimes disincentives. They were then asked to say if they would definitely or might possibly change mode, if these options were available. The results implied modal shifts which, when they were compared to available empirical data (e.g. Ligtermoet, 1998; Schreffler, 1996; FHWA, 1990) appeared to be improbably large. The relativities of the results appeared to be correct, however. Therefore, the coarse results were weighted using Ligtermoet's data. Based on his review of GCPs in the Randstad, Netherlands, he found an average reduction in single occupant car commuting of 5% from schemes consisting mainly of carpooling, 8% from those incorporating financial incentives to use alternative modes, and 15% from those that included financial disincentives to car use.

Table 3.6: Stated preference results (unweighted in brackets)

1.	Scenario C.1-1: provision of preferential parking places for 3 or more car poolers would attract a about 5% (34%) of solo car users to car pooling.
2.	Scenario C.1-2: provision of preferential parking places for 2 or more car poolers would attract a higher percentage of 6.5% (44%) of solo car users to car pooling.
3.	Scenario C.2.1-1: provision of preferential parking places for all car poolers, while for a solo car drivers, they are required to arrive 15 minutes earlier, would attract about 6.3% (43%) of solo car users to car pooling.
4.	Scenario C.2.1-2: provision of preferential parking places for all car poolers, while for a solo car drivers, they are required to arrive 30 minutes earlier, would attract about 7.2% (49%) of solo car users to car pooling.
5.	Scenario C2.2-1: provision of preferential parking places for all car poolers, while for a solo car drivers, they are required to pay £1 parking charge, would attract about 15% (57%) to car pooling.
6.	Scenario C2.2-2: provision of preferential parking places for all car poolers, while for a solo car drivers, they are required to pay £2 parking charge, would attract about 17.6% (67%) of solo car users to car pooling.
7.	Scenario C2.2-2: provision of preferential parking places for all car poolers, while for a solo car drivers, they are required to pay £3 parking charge, would attract about 19.2% (73%) of solo car users to car pooling.
8.	Scenario C2.3-1: provision of preferential parking places for all car poolers, while for a solo car drivers, they are required to pay £1 parking charge, and were given £1 travel allowance. This option would attract about 10% (45%) of solo car users to car pooling.
9.	Scenario C2.3-2: provision of preferential parking places for all car poolers, while for a solo car drivers, they are required to pay £2 parking charge, and were given £2 travel allowance. This option would attract about 10.4% (47%) of solo car users to car pooling.
10.	Scenario C2.3-3: provision of preferential parking places for all car poolers, while for a solo car drivers, they are required to pay £3 parking charge, and were given £3 travel allowance. This option would attract about 13.1% (59%) to car pooling.
11.	Scenario C4-1: provision of preferential parking places for all car poolers, while for a solo car drivers, they are required to pay £1 parking charge, and public transport is 50% cheaper. This option would attract about 15% (43%) of solo car users to car pooling.
12.	Scenario C4-2: provision of preferential parking places for all car poolers, while for a solo car drivers, they are required to pay £2 parking charge, and public transport is 50% cheaper. This option would attract about 17.8% (51%) of solo car users to car pooling.
13.	Scenario C4-3: provision of preferential parking places for all car poolers, while for a solo car drivers, they are required to pay £3 parking charge, and public transport is 50% cheaper. This option would attract about 21.3% (61%) of solo car users to car pooling.
14.	Scenario C5-1: Interest free loans for PT season tickets. This option would attract about 5% (12%) of solo car users to use public transport.
15.	Scenario C5-2: PT is 50% cheaper than currently. This option would attract about 8% (35%) of solo car users to use public transport.
16.	Scenario C6-1: Van-pooling scheme, with charges of £1 per day. This would attract 5% of solo car users.
17.	Scenario C6-2: Van-pooling scheme, with charges of £2 per day. This would attract 3.8% of solo car users.

3.18.2 Elasticities

It was not possible from this stated preference exercise to estimate modal choice models or direct elasticities, because of limited amount of data collected in each scenario. However, it was possible to estimate a unique measure for the effectiveness of each of GCPs from the above data (see Saleh, 1998, Çelikel and Saleh, 2000). These measures of effectiveness have been estimated for each scenario, to be able to compare all scenarios, and can be used as a proxy for elasticity. From these calculations, it appears that the most effective measure is Scenario 3, scoring a relative 22.80. This scenario is the introduction of a £3 per day parking charge at the workplace as well as the provision of (free) car pooling spaces. The least effective scenario was scenario C-1, scoring 10.7, which is provision of parking places for car poolers of 3 people or more, with no disincentive to solo car use.

The SP work has shown, therefore, that the introduction of more interventionist – and costly – measures could have a much more significant impact on the numbers of staff who drive alone to work at HP currently. However, interviews with managers and staff indicate that these measures are likely to remain hypothetical for the foreseeable future.

3.19 Staff Travel Survey 1999, and Comparison with 1997 results

A key reason for choosing Hewlett Packard as a research site for this work was that, prior to the start of the project, it had already (in November 1997) carried out a survey of its staffs' current travel patterns to work and their attitudes to commuting. Thus baseline data was available, against which the effect of the GCP could be measured. To do this, a further staff travel survey was carried out in November 1999.

The survey instrument used was a self-completion questionnaire, illustrated in Appendix 3.7. This was designed in consultation with HP staff and with the client. Major differences to the 1997 survey include the following:

- Inclusion of a detailed question about shift patterns.
- Journey time and distance written in by respondents rather than in bands.
- A question asking if people change mode seasonally, as this can affect parking demand.
- A question asking if people had changed mode since 1997 and, if so, the reason for this.
- A question asking people to give their awareness of and rate the effectiveness of certain HP GCP measures.

About 1300 questionnaires were distributed and 683 returned. These were then entered in a Microsoft Access database. A full and detailed analysis of 1999 results and comparison of these with the 1997 results is contained in Appendix 3.6. The key results for the purposes of this study are that the proportion of people driving alone to work at HP fell from 64% in 1997 to 59% in 1999. While this does not meet the original target for modal shift – a ten percentage point reduction in the proportion of staff driving alone - set in the 1997 GCP, it is a significant step on the way to doing so. This change was because of a statistically significant increase in the proportion of people taking the train: 13% of staff now use it. In spite of the promotion of carsharing, the proportion of people using this mode *fell* over the same period, as some converted to train.

Ninety-three (93) respondents recorded that they had recently changed mode, 16 (73%) of them said they did so in response to a specific HP initiative. Over 37% cited reasons such as reduced cost (36), reduced stress (35) and reduced journey times were mentioned by 23% (21), which can be inferred to relate to the promotion of rail use that has been so central to HP's GCP. Respondents who changed from car on their own to train was, by far, the largest group accounting for 24% of all responses (22 out of 93). This result also relates to a further question, in which respondents were asked to rate the effectiveness of HP's GCP measures in influencing modal shift. Only the rail fares reduction was perceived to be effective.

3.19.1 Implications of survey results for HP GCP

The implications of these results were discussed with the two staff responsible for GCP implementation and maintenance at HP, Michael McBride (Environmental Health and Safety Specialist (EHSS)) and Ian McIntosh (Environmental Health and Safety Manager (EHSM)), on 24th February 2000. Both were extremely pleased with the baseline change which, according to Ian, exceeded his personal expectations (in spite of the original target of a 10% reduction). From this, both staff would like to see "more aggressive" targets set in a new plan. Such a target might be a 15 percentage point reduction in drive alone commuting compared to the 1997 level, to be achieved by 2001. In order to do this, the revised GCP is likely to focus on the following elements:

- Improving cycle facilities still further, probably in tandem with the opening of the new A90 bikepath.
- Review the possibility of running a company bus, for example from Bo'ness and Linlithgow, both of which are very poorly linked by public transport but which have considerable concentrations of staff.
- Feeding back results of the survey to ScotRail and ensuring that the discounted ticket continues. Assisting ScotRail if possible with revenue protection at Dalmeny station. (This is due to a perception that the success of the ticket offer has brought more new passengers to Dalmeny station than ScotRail are able to collect fares from.)
- Continued promotion of the GCP through the new intranet site (see excerpts in Appendix 3.1), through induction, and through periodic promotions.

The parking situation on site and on the northern access road is likely to become more acute. While both interviewees would like to see some subsidy by the company to staff to use alternative modes, they both perceive that this, and any restriction of eligibility for car parking permits, would be unlikely to gain senior management support until all other avenues have been explored. The avenue currently being explored by management, however, is to build and open a new car park to cope with increasing employee numbers.

A further barrier identified by the EHSS is a hardening of attitudes to the GCP. He perceives that many of the staff whose mode choice was relatively easy to influence have changed modes. Amongst the remainder, "transport is in their head" and they have thought through justifications for driving. Hence fewer respondents in the 1999 survey said that they were prepared to carshare compared to 1997.

3.19.2 Conclusion to Chapter Three

This chapter has reviewed the motivations for the implementation of the GCP at HP and shown how the initiative is very much in keeping with HP's strong corporate culture. It has also shown how the various measures which comprise the plan have been selected, and attempted to review the limited evidence available to date of the effects of these measures. The results of the Panel Survey have confirmed the results of the 1997 travel survey, and this has been compared to 1999 data to show that there has been a modal shift *away* from commuting by car. With a view to the future effectiveness of the GCP at HP (now Agilent Technologies) it is important to note that:

- The panel survey, interviews and focus groups have shown that car users do not feel that the elements of the GCP have a great influence on their modal choice.
- The focus groups suggested a range of additional and more effective measures but at present HP does not wish to pursue these, with the possible exception of a company bus.
- The elements chosen for inclusion in the GCP are relatively cheap and non-controversial for the company to implement. They were also implemented extremely quickly. A full business case was not required and there has been in consequence no complete analysis of the costs and benefits of the GCP to date.
- Parking pressure was eased by the construction of a temporary car park and by less intense levels of recruitment during 1998 than there was in 1996-97. This may have made the need for a GCP less pressing at this time. However, this situation is now (February 2000) changing once again.

The senior management interviews carried out at the start of the project certainly revealed a view amongst those managers that the GCP was something they would take so far, but not so far that it required significant resources. Since the GCP has now been shown to have exceeded expectations, it is unlikely that this attitude will change, unless it is not possible to secure additional car parking. Nonetheless, those implementing the GCP are likely to push for more aggressive modal shift targets in a revised plan. Finally it should not be forgotten that the HP case study has shown that Green Commuter Plans can work.

4. CHAPTER FOUR

4.1 Kirkton Campus

Kirkton Campus is a business park on the western edge of Livingston New Town. It is located about 2.5 km to the west of the town centre and about 3.5 km from both Livingston North and Livingston South stations. The former offers a half hourly service and 18 minute journey time to Edinburgh and Bathgate only, while the latter offers an hourly service to Glasgow and Edinburgh - journey times are one hour and half an hour respectively. There is a peak-hour bus link from the Campus to Livingston North, none to Livingston South, and a half-hourly service to Livingston Town Centre (where connections can be made for Edinburgh) and onwards to Shotts.

As Livingston is a New Town, it has been planned around the car and the segregation of the pedestrian and cyclist from motor vehicle traffic. There is an extensive network of cycle/footpaths throughout the town and these serve the Campus, but they are under-used due to personal security concerns. The capacity of the road network is ample except at peak times in certain locations such as the Campus when, anecdotal evidence suggests, it can take as long as 20 minutes to travel along the distributor road to the A705 (see Figure 4.1). The majority of the companies in the Campus perceive that they have adequate parking, although there are some large employers who do not, notably BSkyB. There are others, such as the Royal Bank of Scotland Statement Dispatch centre, who are unable to recruit staff who do not have a car, since alternative means of travel to the area are so poor.

The local authority, West Lothian Council, has recently granted planning permission for the construction of a new R+D facility for the American software company, Cadence. This will bring an additional 2000 jobs to the Campus by the year 2001, and will also sever the route of a planned link road which would have provided additional capacity to permit easy access and egress to and from the Campus at peak times. Hence the Council has become anxious to promote green commuting in the area so that congestion does not threaten its economic vitality. In total in the Campus there are some 49 companies, 21 of which employ more than 50 people. Companies range in size from those with fewer than 10 employees at one end of the spectrum, to BSkyB with 5,000 at the other (though not all of these are full-time). In total about 7,000 people currently work on the Campus.

Given the actual and potential problems of traffic congestion in the area, West Lothian Council and the Scottish Executive jointly funded a consultant, Ben Ireland (BICS), to contact all the companies in the area with a view to setting up a Green Commuter Forum of the campus' employers. This Forum could then lobby transport providers and work together to promote and perhaps provide better alternative forms of transport to the area. BICS also visited 18 of the 21 larger employers in the area to discuss their concerns with green commuting, and 25 of all employers contacted completed a short questionnaire summarising their transport problems and their potential interest in a Green Commuter Forum. A report of the discussions and the survey are presented in Appendix 4.1, so it is not intended to duplicate them in full here. However, in terms of the model of GCP development set out in Chapter Two, most of the organisations in the campus (perhaps with the exception of Cadence) were in the pre-contemplation stage. BICS' visits were intended to move them into the contemplation phase.

Figure 4.1: Map of Kirkton Campus Area

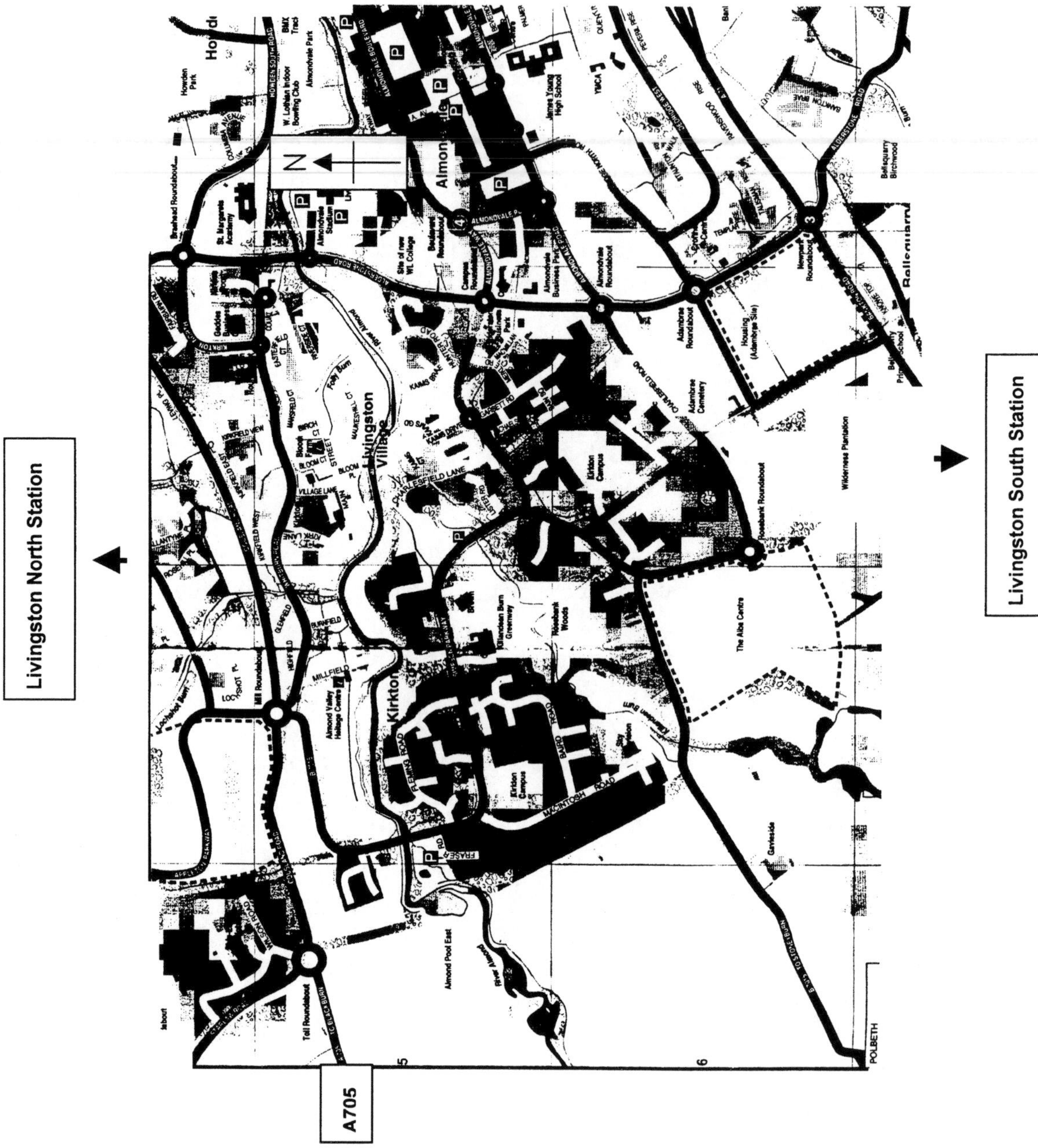

4.2 Green Commuting Forum - Meetings Held, Attendance and Results

A key objective of the research was to monitor the effectiveness of a Kirkton Campus Green Commuting Forum – essentially intended to bring companies in the Campus together to work on green commuting issues. An inaugural meeting was held in January 1999, attended by about 18 companies, though in some cases deputies were sent rather than the original invitee. It had been hoped by the Council that a leader for the Forum would come forward at the meeting, but in the event, no-one was prepared to assume this role, and so instead it was agreed that a further meeting would be convened by the local Chamber of Commerce.

Subsequent meetings in April and July, convened by and held at the offices of West Lothian Chamber of Commerce (WLCOC), were attended by 5 and 2 companies respectively. At the latter meeting, interim results of the Kirkton Campus travel survey were presented and subsequently posted to all companies in the campus. It was notable at both later meetings that the companies present were reluctant to take a lead in maintaining the Green Commuter Forum and were rather looking for assistance and guidance from the Napier University research team; however, the team felt that their role had to be kept to that of monitoring rather than assisting, though they referred companies to the free advice and consultancy available from the DETR Energy and Environment Best Practice Phoneline. A further meeting took place on October 6th, 1999, when West Lothian Council's Head of Public Transport presented a new Kirkton Campus public transport guide (see Appendix 4.2). Once again, only two employers were present at the meeting.

4.2.1 Kirkton Campus Staff Travel Survey

At the meeting on 14 April 1999 it was agreed to issue staff travel questionnaire forms to twelve companies. These forms were designed and issued by WLCOC and completed forms returned to them. WLCOC then passed them to Napier University for coding and analysis.

It is very important to note that no responses from BskyB, by far the largest company in the campus, were ever received. The first 500 survey forms posted to them were mislaid; a further 500 were forwarded to them in August and the responses are still awaited. Given the significance of BSkyB as an employer on the Campus, it is unfortunate that it has been so difficult to obtain responses from them. Several approaches were required to obtain completed forms from several other companies. In general, it did not appear that the travel survey was a high priority for some of the companies surveyed. At the end of October 1999, from ten of the twelve employers (not including BSkyB) surveyed, 381 responses had been received, representing about 5% of the employees at the Campus. However, 25 "late" responses were received from an eleventh company (not BSkyB). In February 2000 a further 45 responses were also received from a company not originally surveyed! This brought the total number of responses up to a total of 451 (see Table 4.1).

Table 4.1: Response totals and percentages by company

Company	Number of responses	%age of total
Award plc	25	6%
Banta Global Turnkey	34	7%
Bioscot Ltd	3	1%
Edinburgh Sensors	12	3%
Ethicon Ltd	174	39%
Flexco Packaging Ltd	12	3%
Magnum Power Solutions Ltd	14	3%
Quintiles Scotland Ltd	46	10%
Scottish Coal	23	5%
Serologicals Ltd	45	10%
Silva UK Production Ltd	29	6%
The Royal Bank of Scotland plc	34	8%
All Companies	**451**	**100%**

One company - Ethicon Ltd - contributed 174 responses (39% of the total) and it was - by far - the largest single return received. Quintiles Scotland Ltd contributed 46 (10%) returns and Bioscot Ltd assisted with 3 (1%).

It is important to note that the travel survey was a relatively "quick and dirty" method of gathering basic travel data and attitudes from employees in the campus. As such it has some methodological flaws, which are highlighted in the text. Nonetheless it is an important initial step in baseline data gathering and in raising awareness of green commuting issues.

4.2.2 Usual mode of travel to work

Table 4.2 shows the usual mode of travel to work for all companies surveyed. The majority (64%) of staff travel to work in their own car unaccompanied. A quarter (25%) either carshare or take a lift with colleagues (the distinction between carsharing and getting a lift with or without payment may have been unclear to respondents). Buses – either minibuses or scheduled – account in total for 10% of travel. Other modes (eg walking, cycling or train) do not feature largely. For the eleven companies surveyed the car is associated with 89% of trips – a figure well in excess of the national UK average (see Table 4.4).

Table 4.2 Usual mode of travel by number, percentage and average distance				
Mode	Number	%	UK 1996 mode,%	Distance, Kirkton
Car, on your own.	286	64		14.6
Car, passenger.	63	14	70	6.3
Car, sharing.	48	11		9.8
Bus.	25	6	8	9.0
Other: Minibus.	14	3	-	9.6
Bicycle.	7	2	4	5.9
Walk.	5	1	12	1.8
Other: Bus then lift.	1	0	2	8.6
Train.	1	0	3	14.7
Missing.	1	0	-	-
All modes	**451**	**100**		**12.2**
Average distance is based on actual average distance calculated from equivalent bands in the 1999 Hewlett Packard travel survey as shown in Table 4.3.				

The data in Table 4.2 indicate that people working in Kirkton Campus travel an average of 12.2 miles to get to work (on the assumption that distance band averages are similar to those calculated for the Hewlett Packard data). Average distance by travel mode is shown and it can be seen that those who travel by car unaccompanied travel further (14.6 miles) than average. Carsharing distances tend to be longer (9.8 miles) than getting a lift (6.3 miles). At just under 10 miles average distances, bus and minibus travel are of broadly similar lengths to carsharing and rather more than the average for getting a lift. As expected cycling and walking tend to be over shorter distances (5.9 and 1.8 miles respectively. [Care must be taken in such an interpretation because the distinction between carsharing and being a car passenger may not have been clear to respondents].

As indicated in Table 4.2, the usual mode of transport is by car unaccompanied (64% of all responses) but this does vary by company. Up to 80% of staff in some companies (eg Quintiles Scotland Ltd) travel by car unaccompanied – in other companies (eg Silva UK Production Ltd) equivalent figures are in the 40-50% range. This may reflect a recent relocation of premises or the need for specialist staff necessarily recruited on a "non-local" basis.

As indicated in Table 4.3, the overall average travel to work distance is 12.2 miles and it does vary by company. The distribution of the statistical mode[5] (ie most commonly recorded distance band) displays this. The statistical mode for Banta Global Turnkey is 2-5 miles whereas the equivalent value for Quintiles and Scottish Coal is over 20 miles.

Table 4.3: Journey to work by company, distance band and average distance[1]

Company	Distance band (miles)						Total	Average distance
	<= 1	1 – 2	2 - 5	5 - 10	10 - 20	> 20		
Magnum Power Solutions Ltd	0	0	0	1	4	9	14	26.9
Scottish Coal	0	2	3	1	3	14	23	23.9
Quintiles Scotland Ltd	3	1	11	4	10	17	46	17.8
Bioscot Ltd	0	0	2	0	0	1	3	14.3
Serologicals Ltd	4	2	15	4	8	12	45	14.1
Award plc	1	5	6	5	3	5	25	11.8
Edinburgh Sensors	1	2	3	0	5	1	12	10.4
Flexco Packaging Ltd	0	0	4	5	2	1	12	10.3
Ethicon Ltd	8	15	51	52	29	18	173	10.1
Silva UK Production Ltd	0	4	10	8	4	2	28	8.8
Banta Global Turnkey	0	7	14	6	5	2	34	7.8
The Royal Bank of Scotland plc	2	8	13	4	5	2	34	7.3
No distance stated							2	-
All Companies	19	46	132	90	78	84	451	12.2

[1] Average distance is based on actual average distance calculated from equivalent bands in the 1999 Hewlett Packard travel survey.

Shaded values indicate statistical mode (most commonly occurring value)

Reasons why the statistical modes and averages differ may relate to:

the relocation of a company - where a company moves its plant/offices to a new location within a reasonable travelling distance it is likely that the majority of staff members will continue – at least in the short/medium term – in employment with that company. This will involve individual staff members changing travel arrangements from a personally chosen place of employment to one "imposed" on them. Consequently travel to work trips may be longer and not so convenient by public transport as before.

the degree of specialisation of staff profiles – if a company requires highly specialised staff it may require to recruit an employ people over a wider area than would be necessary for less specialised staff. Specialist staff are likely to enjoy higher salaries and are prepared – in return – to travel further and to afford to do so by car if public transport is not a convenient option.

As might be expected, there is a significant correlation between the average distance to work by company and the proportion of staff in a company who travel to work by car unaccompanied. Table 4.4 summarises this where the Spearman's Rank Correlation Test z score of 2.099 is significant ($p<0.05$: critical value for z is 1.96 at the 5% level).

The rightmost three columns of Table 4.7 provide very brief details of each company's position regarding relocation and staff specialisation. It can be seen that – with the exception of Scottish Coal – companies with longer average travel to work distances and proportions of unaccompanied car use tend either to be recently relocated at Kirkton Campus and/or have a high need for specialist staff.

---

[5] The term "statistical mode" is used here to distinguish it from mode of travel.

Table 4.4: Spearman's Rank Correlation Test for correlation between average distance to work and percentage traveling by car unaccompanied

Company	Average distance	Rank	%age car user on own	Rank	D^2	Years at Kirkton Campus	New/ relocate	Requirement for specialist staff
Magnum Power Solutions Ltd	26.9	1	79	2	1	4	relocate	high
Scottish Coal	23.9	2	74	5	9	2.5	relocate	medium*
Quintiles Scotland Ltd	17.8	3	80	1	4	4	relocate	high
Serologicals Ltd	14.1	4	76	3	1	1	relocate	medium
Award plc	11.8	5	52	9	16	5	new	medium
Edinburgh Sensors	10.4	6	75	4	4	0.5	relocate	high/medium
Flexco Packaging Ltd	10.3	7	50	10	9	3	new	low
Ethicon Ltd	10.1	8	59	7	1	>5	-	low
Silva UK Production Ltd	8.8	9	45	11	4	>5	-	medium
Banta Global Turnkey	7.8	10	68	6	16	>3	new	high
The Royal Bank of Scotland plc	7.3	11	56	8	9	2	relocate	low
Sum of rank differences squared					74			
Spearman's Rank Correlation Test: z score					2.099			

D^2 is the square of the difference between ranks
* Scottish Coal may experience high staff retention because of the nature of its business, preserved salaries and generous pensions

This not an unexpected result. Nonetheless, it could have important consequences particularly where companies are relocating and intending either to retain a large proportion of their existing staff or to recruit for new highly specialised staff. Such situations are likely to lead to a greater reliance on car-based travel and this may be a matter of concern to a local planning authority.

4.2.3 Occasional modes of travel to work when usual mode is not available

Respondents were asked to indicate no more than two occasional modes of travel. Where two occasional modes were recorded – or more than two as was sometimes the case - it is not clear whether such responses refer to alternatives (eg walk or bus) or to joint use of modes (eg walk and bus on a single journey).

For car commuters who travel on their own, the largest group of responses (42%) say that no alternative transport mode is used. A further 27% indicate that they would travel as a car passenger. Carshare and bus are each quoted by 12% of respondents as occasional modes. In total, therefore, over 80% of people travelling to work unaccompanied in a car indicate that their alternative travel arrangement(s) includes a car-based trip.

The position is rather different for car passengers where the largest group of between a quarter and a third (29%) use a bus as their alternative mode. A further 23% indicate that they would walk. The third biggest group (16%) would cycle. Some of these respondents may either not own a car or do not possess a driving licence and it would, therefore, be wrong to assume that all travel choices were available.

The largest groups (25% each) of carsharers indicate that they would either continue to carshare (by stating "No alternative transport used") or travel by car on their own. Nearly one in five (19%) each quote car passenger, bus or walk as alternative modes. In total, therefore, almost 70% of carsharers indicate that their alternative travel arrangement(s) includes a car-based trip.

Over three-quarters (76%) of bus users say that they would travel as a car passenger (52%) or as a carsharer (24%). One in six respondents (16%) indicated that they would get to work by car on their own. In total, therefore, over 90% of bus users indicate that their alternative travel arrangement(s) includes a car-based trip. This may suggest that at least some of the people who use the bus do so in preference – for whatever reason – to using a car or, as indicated above, do not possess a driving licence.

Most (71%) cyclists report that their alternative travel arrangement(s) includes a car-based trip (The number of cyclists in the sample was 7 and it would, therefore, be unreasonable to place much emphasis on this observation).

4.2.4 Encouragement to use (or continue to use) public transport

Respondents were asked to indicate what changes would encourage use of public transport. A "tick list" was provided and respondents were asked to tick no more than two: in the event, several respondents ticked more than two and the average number of changes recorded was 2.12/respondent. The provision of more direct bus routes was seen by almost three-quarters (72%) of all usual mode groups to be the most important change that would encourage use of public transport. This is perhaps not surprising given that the focus groups there clearly identified lack of direct routes to the Campus as a major barrier to public transport use.

Improvements in frequency and reliability was the second most quoted change at a 60% response rate again by all groups alike. More frequent/reliable train services and better public transport information – each at a 10% response rate – were not viewed by many as being an encouragement to use public transport.

4.2.5 Willingness to carshare

Respondents were asked if they were prepared to car share and, if so, whether with a colleague or with someone from a company nearby. One third of the forms showed a no response: it is not possible determine whether these relate to an unwillingness to carshare, inability to decide or simply to an omission.

Of people who did respond, by far the most common response (71% overall) was a willingness to share with a colleague. The next most common response although at the very much lower response rate of 17% was sharing with a colleague or with someone from a company nearby. Interestingly, people whose usual mode is car-based show a greater preparedness to share only with a colleague whereas bus users are much more prepared to carshare also with someone from a company nearby.

4.2.6 Arrival and departure times

An analysis of arrivals and departures by time of day shows a pattern rather different to that of the standard 9 to 5. The busy times may relate to the start or end of a shift and especially where there is an overlap of staff arriving and departing. The busiest times of day include 8 am and 5 pm, but also 2 pm, 10 pm and around 4 pm. It is interesting to note that three of the busiest ten times are during the evening peak and that busy times in the morning are more spread out.

These varied times obviously have implications for the ability of people in the campus to car share with those from other companies

If this sample is representative – and there are doubts about this because of the lack of BSkyB data – then the numbers could be multiplied by about ten to give an indication of total movements of people. Businesses may be able to use this type of information to lobby bus (and rail) companies for more frequent and better targeted bus services.

4.2.7 Council area of employees' address

Table 4.11 shows that two thirds (67%) of employees live in West Lothian and that Edinburgh at 14% is the next largest source of staff. Just under one in five (19%) live elsewhere. This may indicate that better designed local public transport services could have a role to play in changing mode to bus.

4.3 Selection of Representative Companies at Kirkton Campus

To achieve a spread of company size it was decided to approach three companies who had expressed an interest or willingness to assist in the research. 4.5 lists the three companies together with staff numbers. The companies indicated a willingness to be involved.

Table 4.5 : Companies at Kirkton Campus involved in Study

Company	Number of Staff
Sky	3,000
Quintiles	200
Royal Bank of Scotland plc	40

It is important to be aware that the panels were effectively self selected by a combination of the company and individual staff member. Although this selection method may lead to a bias in the representation of all staff in the companies concerned. As the purpose of the panel is to monitor and track change in attitudes following ongoing exposure to green commuting initiatives implemented in their workplace, any bias in the staff sample is not considered to damage the main thrust of this part of the project.

4.4 Senior Management Interviews

It was possible to arrange only two senior management interviews, one at Quintiles, with the Director of Human Resources (DHR), and one at the Royal Bank of Scotland, with Operations Manager (OM). The interview schedule used is appended (Appendix 4.3). If it is compared to the interview schedule used for key managers at HP, it will be noted that there are, of necessity, fewer questions regarding green commuting *per se* and that those that remain are inevitably largely hypothetical. While this may have made it difficult for the interviewees at KC to comment on the effect of individual green commuting measures, they were able to talk in principle about the way in which a GCP might be implemented within their organisation.

It was intended to carry out further interviews with the facilities manager at each site and with managers at Sky but, ultimately, it proved impossible to arrange these. Those senior manager interviews that were carried out were not repeated because no green commuting measures were implemented in the Campus during the lifetime of the project and thus there was little further that these managers could comment upon.

4.5 Quintiles

Quintiles' main business is to develop and test new pharmaceutical products for major clients. Quintiles (Scotland) Ltd currently employs 450 staff at its Riccarton site, 350 in Bathgate and 200 at its two adjacent sites in Kirkton Campus, from a total workforce worldwide of about 21,000. The Scottish operation is set for a major expansion that will affect the Kirkton Campus sites.

Quintiles employs scientific, technical, administrative and operator staff so its recruitment can range from the local – one HR specialist noted that many jobs at Kirkton are advertised locally, partly because of transport problems to the site – to the trans-national. The same HR specialist was lamenting the difficulty of recruiting Lithuanian and Italian speakers. A limited number of staff work shifts but these are unpredictable as they are related to the nature of the current contract on which they are working. This obviously has implications for their transport requirements.

The transport problems suffered by the staff at the Kirkton site relate to on-site parking and local congestion, in the main. The former is limited in that on one of the Quintiles sites there is an excess of parking but staff at the other adjacent site, where parking is in short supply, are unwilling to walk 200 metres from the empty car park. The latter occurs only at BSkyB shift changeover times.

Some 127 staff have recently transferred from Riccarton and they have more acute transport problems, particularly if they are carless and live in Edinburgh. In recognition of these difficulties, the DHR said that the company had investigated the cost of a contract bus from Edinburgh but that the cost had been prohibitive; and that approaches to local public transport providers for improved services to the Campus had not borne fruit. The staff who have transferred receive an allowance (declining over time) in recognition of the additional costs they have to bear on their new commute. However, the DHR would be reluctant to go beyond this level of intervention in staff travel to work, believing that it is largely the responsibility of the individual to ensure that they can get there. Car-sharing is "encouraged", but no active mechanism is used to do so.

The DHR was of the opinion that staff would be oblivious to the fact that there is any kind of green commuting initiative in the campus; if green commuting is associated with anything, it is with the bus services which are perceived as wholly inadequate and expensive. From a management point of view, he believes that green commuting will only be taken up by an employer like Quintiles if there is a business case for it.

There would be a business case if considerable numbers of (especially more specialist) staff have problems in getting to work, and if this begins to affect recruitment and retention, as this would become a cost to the business. In his opinion, Quintiles does not currently suffer transport-related recruitment problems, and in exit interviews for staff who are leaving, transport problems do not feature as even a contributory factor to their decision to move on. The physical space and grants available for locating at Kirkton Campus far outweighed any slight disadvantages due to its relatively poor accessibility by modes other than the private car and, as the DHR noted,

> *"High quality staff recruitment is not a transport issue because they travel by car. Edinburgh is a magnet for good staff and recruitment from Europe is not uncommon."*

A certain number of what might be termed green transport measures are already in place. The company uses teleconferencing to reduce travel between its sites. It also has staff who work from home some or all of the time, because this suits them and the company. Cycle provision is also being increased at the Riccarton site, though not at Kirkton, where he perceives that there is no demand from staff for such facilities. But in each case the implementation of these measures is driven by a business need, not by green transport considerations or a desire to improve the "greater good". The company operates as a group of teams working on specific contracts for specific customers and it is driven by these customer imperatives; thus staff transport is *not* a priority unless it threatens the organisation's ability to meet these imperatives which, at present, it does not. Thus Quintiles' active participation in green commuting initiatives at the campus would appear to be unlikely at this stage.

4.6 Royal Bank of Scotland

The Royal Bank's statement despatch centre employs 40 staff on 3 shifts (0500-1300; 0700-1500; and 0800-1600) and sends out about 3 million items of post per month. However this is set to increase and by September 2000 there will be 55 staff and a 24 hour operation. There is a mixture of direct bank employees and staff on agency contracts; for both, however, staff turnover is low and rates of pay are above average for this type of work in this area.

Staff travel problems are limited to those who do not own a car and are unable to get a lift to work, as the bus service does not meet their needs due to start and finish times and, usually, a need to change in Livingston centre. However, there is a strong culture of lift giving and staff help each other to get to work. There are no parking problems, and congestion problems are limited to Sky's start and finish times. Informal covered cycle parking is available in the loading bay. When new staff are recruited, the agency is told that only those staff who are able to get to the site should be sent for jobs; this has never led to a post being unfilled.

The Operations Manager was firmly of the opinion that the primary responsibility for encouraging green commuting lay with central and local government, and that they needed to vastly improve public transport. While the OM saw a limited role for employers in, say, providing contract buses, he believed that this would be difficult to negotiate if shared between companies. Most of all he felt that to get involved in transport provision layout outwith the scope of his job; his primary responsibility is to ensure that statements are despatched to target and to keep costs down, and he has no time to do much else.

The major barrier to more companies engaging in green commuting is the lack of organisational priority accorded to it and that this is related to its cost. For the Operations Manager, it would be difficult to justify to his manager spending money on contract buses or even cycle parking, although (if there was time) it would be possible to more actively organise car sharing, perhaps with adjacent companies, and also to group together with other local employers to lobby for better public transport services. However, at present, this is not a priority because the centre's staff do not suffer significant transport problems. The informal culture of the organisation ensures that lifts are arranged easily, even when unexpected overtime occurs or when people need to get home in an emergency. Staff are rarely left stranded.

Thus from both the Royal Bank and Quintiles, there is a strong message that green commuting is *not* a business priority and that it will only become so if it starts to threaten the operation of the core business.

4.7 Panel Travel Survey

It was agreed as part of the contract for the research project to undertake more detailed investigations into company and staff attitudes in Kirkton Campus regarding green commuting and also to seek information on travel behaviour and actions. Unlike at Hewlett Packard no management-led green commuting initiatives have been launched in the campus. In order to allow for comparison between companies, questionnaire forms almost identical to those used at HP were issued to the selected companies in Kirkton Campus (a copy of this questionnaire form is shown Appendix 4.4).

Fifty responses were received from the three companies concerned. The Human Resources Manager at Quintiles indicated that he had trawled the staff twice for volunteers he was only able to receive eleven returns. Table 4.6 summarises the returns.

Table 4.6: Respondents by Company and Sex				
Company	Number of Staff	Female	Male	All
Sky	3,000	12	6	18
Quintiles	200	8	3	11
Royal Bank of Scotland plc	40	8	13	21
All	-	28	22	50

4.7.1 Characteristics of panel members

In comparison to HP, the panel members at Kirkton Campus are younger, more likely to be female, to have a family, and to be without a driving licence, and they live (even) more locally. This may be a reflection of lower rates of pay in many of the jobs in the Campus compared to HP. Younger people – particularly in the age range 25-34 – form half the sample. Over half (58%) of the panellists live in West Lothian; Edinburgh accounts for one in five, and the remainder live within the former Strathclyde Region area.

4.7.2 Travel patterns

Mode of travel is shown in Table 4.7. Compared to the KC travel survey, a lower proportion of panel members drives alone. This reflects the self-selected nature of the sample.

50

Table 4.7: Mode of travel to work

Mode of travel	Number	%age
Car share	24	48
Car (not sharing)	20	40
Not stated	2	4
Minibus	2	4
Motorcycle	1	2
Unknown	1	2
All modes	**50**	**100**

It is notable that minibus is used by a small proportion: in the absence of convenient and affordable public transport, workers on fixed shifts have organised their own. On average, panel members spend some £13 per week on transport to work; car sharing and the minibus were the most affordable modes.

The factors which influence choice of mode are shown below in Table 4.8. The average values for the factors require careful interpretation because they do not necessarily represent the "performance" of the factor but rather the view of its influence in mode choice. However, they do indicate that convenience, reliability and cost are all important influences on modal choice for those who drive or carshare to work.

Table 4.8: Average strength of interest of travel factors by car commute

Factor influencing mode choice for journey to work	Commute by car?	Number of Responses	Average of Response[1]
(a) This is the shortest travel time for home-work journey.	No	6	4.67
	Yes	42	6.10
(b) This is the most reliable mode.	No	6	5.67
	Yes	40	5.85
(c) Cost of this mode is lower than via an alternative mode.	No	6	4.83
	Yes	40	4.63
(d) This mode allows for non-work related stops to be made en-route.	No	6	2.00
	Yes	39	4.10
(e) Irregular working hours are a feature of my position.	No	7	4.14
	Yes	39	4.31
(f) This mode is the safest form of travel to/from work.	No	6	3.00
	Yes	39	4.00
(g) There is a walk exceeding 10 minutes from my home to the nearest bus/rail halt.	No	6	2.83
	Yes	33	3.33

[1]Response ranged from 1=least influence to 7=greatest influence

When commenting on their modal choice, many panel members amplified these reasons. In particular, the perceived complexity of the public transport alternative was highlighted. Panel members also stressed the lack of public transport services at times that coincide with work start times.

Panel members were also asked to suggest measures that would assist in promoting travel by "greener" modes of transport. While a few suggested cycle facilities at the workplace, the vast majority stressed instead the need for "better" public transport – although the degree of improvement required was not stated. This perception of transport as an issue *external* to the organisation was reinforced when panel members were asked to rate the influence that GCP measures would have on their travel habits. For car users, all measures that their employer could implement (bar one – cheaper public transport fares) were perceived to have no potential influence.

4.8 Panel Interviews

Panel interviews were not undertaken at Kirkton Campus, as it was felt that, in the absence of the implementation of any GCP measures, this would be repeating the data gathering exercises of the panel survey and the focus groups.

4.9 Panel Focus Groups

The Kirkton Focus Groups Schedule is shown in Appendix 4.5. Here, in contrast to HP, the emphasis was on personal issues and perceptions relating to green commuting. As no staff had been formally exposed to the issues through their employer, the organisational issues - which were a feature of the Hewlett Packard groups - were not specifically addressed. However, an attempt was made to introduce the concept of the employer encouraging green commuting, and to ask staff whether they thought this was both a justifiable activity and one in which their employer was ever likely to engage.

The Kirkton Focus Groups were held over three days as follows:

Company	Date	Time	Number in group
Sky	31 August 1999	13.00-14.00	9
Quintiles	1 September 1999	11.00-12.00	7
Royal Bank of Scotland	2 September 1999	11.00-12.00	8
Royal Bank of Scotland	2 September 1999	12.00-13.00	6

4.9.1 Choice of Mode

The general mood of the focus groups was one of frustration regarding the poor transport provision to the area. One person went as far as to say, *"I resent having to buy a car to get to work"*, and another referred to Kirkton Campus as a *"God forsaken place"*.

Attendees were unanimous about the extremely poor level of public transport provision and a kind of *siege spirit* was evident in a number of comments received. Bus connections:

- are slow, expensive and infrequent, and the times not convenient for company start times
- invariably require a change at Livingston Bus Station
- and do not allow their use at lunchtime or for other visits (doctor/dentist etc)

One focus group participant who lives outside Bathgate (9 miles away) calculated that to get to work by bus on time, her journey time would be 3 times longer than by car and it would cost her £15 per day (including a taxi for a part of the journey). The significant majority of employees, therefore, felt – often quite reluctantly - that the only realistic option was to travel by car either by own car or taking a lift. Reasons, therefore, for using a car are often justified not on the virtues of a car but on the total lack of an acceptable alternative. Comments also related to the lack of good and/or secure paths for pedestrians and cyclists and also the lack of facilities for them at the place of work. This discourages the use of those modes. The following comments illustrate some of these problems.

"Only local people would cycle."

"You can't get a bus to here from Bathgate before 9.00am."

"I like the car because of the security angle."

"I couldn't nip home at lunchtime to do the hoovering {without a car)"

In general it was quite difficult to disentangle modal choice from the discussion of problems getting to and from work.

4.9.2 Commuting problems

The groups generally all identified the same problems and this was perhaps the most animated area of discussion. This issue very much overlaps with the earlier issue of how people get to work.

For those who drive or car-share, the major problems relate to road congestion, difficulties in finding a parking space, different start/end times (for sharing) and car-sharer dependency on other people.   These problems often mean people adapt to the circumstances by making adjustments to their travel habits:

"Working late to avoid congestion becomes a habit. It's a culture here and it has to be broken."

"At 5.00pm it's a nightmare: Sky2 comes out and you're delayed at the Mill Roundabout for 20 minutes."

"You can't leave at lunch time because can't get a parking space when you return."

However, it is important to note that the problems of congestion and parking were largely limited to employees at Sky, to those who use major trunk roads such as the A720 and M8 to get to work, and those Quintiles staff who had recently relocated from Edinburgh.   Other staff do not find getting to work a problem; local roads are rarely congested (with the exception of the Mill Roundabout to the north) and there is sufficient parking at work.   At the Royal Bank, where car-sharing is commonplace, most staff reported the arrangements to be reliable but at the same time quite flexible.   Very few staff use public transport but reported significant problems of cost, long journey times, inconvenient interchange, unreliability and exposure to the elements on those occasions when they tried to or were forced to use it.

4.9.3 Is there a need for Greener Travel habits?

Good alternatives to the use of a car were seen as important but more as providing a choice which might be cheaper rather than as an opportunity to use greener forms of transport.

"I thought travel to Kirkton Campus would be OK but was disappointed when I got the timetables."

"I wish there was a bus - I could read a paper."

There was, however, an appreciation of the wider issues involved:

"Less cars more space gives better use of land."

Overall, there was a perception of a need to green travel habits, but employees who personally suffered the greatest problems were perhaps more committed to the idea, and the primary responsibility for making transport greener was seen to lie with the Government rather than with individuals or, significantly, employers.

4.9.4 Problems with greener transport

Significant concerns were expressed about the facilities for pedestrians, cyclists and bus users and the general mood was not one of optimism. Many of the justifications for using the car to get to work were closely linked to problems with greener transport. Several participants had either used public transport previously, or had made the effort to find out about services to the Campus, but had found these services inadequate and/or too expensive.

"It's not a place built for pedestrians - you don't see a lot of pedestrians walking about."

"Bus fares are high it's £1.70 single from Bathgate - £3.40 return!"

"I've seen more bikes than before and it's nice. They could upgrade the cycle paths."

There was a strong feeling that staff valued their time extremely highly and did not therefore want to spend another one and a half hours per day using a greener mode of transport to get to work. The lack of direct and/or integrated services pushes up public transport journey times relative to the car and is therefore a significant deterrent.

4.9.5 Could and should employers help promote greener transport?

The comments received in answer to this area of the discussion have to be read with the caveat that this was really the first time that employees had ever been exposed to the concept of their employer encouraging the use of greener modes of travel to work. It was necessary for the focus group facilitator to describe some of the initiatives taken by other local companies, particularly those in west Edinburgh.

There was a general view that the companies could and should be doing something but there was a feeling that it would all make little difference. Some panellists referred to increasing difficulties as planned new developments in the campus come on line. (*"The area's going to get busier yet with Quintiles having another 1,500 workers."*)

Suggestions for fairly generic GCP measures included cycle parking and showers, formalised carsharing schemes with parking incentives, and lobbying bus operators. There were however two more specific ideas:

> *"I travel in a 14 seat minibus - £10 a week - I don't see why Sky and the Council couldn't organise it and possibly subsidise it."*

> *"A Sky minibus would be a good idea from Livingston North station."*

There was however some doubt that companies would be willing to expend resources on many of these facilities. At Sky, participants felt that their employer was benefiting from the transport problems suffered by its employees: staff get in early and stay late in order to beat the rush, and consequently spend more time at work for no extra pay. This was perceived to be a barrier to the company promoting greener transport. It was summed up in two comments received:

> *"They get an extra hour out of staff (<08.00 and >17.00) and also tied to the desk at lunchtime."*

> *"I share with three others from Glasgow for cost reasons but it is also good because I have to leave (when my car shares do) - it's not popular with management."*

Some panellists also pointed out some potential advantages there would be to their employer particularly in areas of recruitment and staff retention:

> *"A lot of people are put off working at Kirkton Campus - some young people don't have driving licences."*

> *"Staff are well trained and are poached - so they're could be a benefit to entice them to stay."*

In summary, there was a desire from staff to see their employer take a more active role in promoting and facilitating more travel options for their staff, but some doubt - especially at Sky - that their employer would be willing to devote resources to this.

4.9.6 Commonalities and Differences Between Companies

The Kirkton Campus Focus Group results have shown that there is support among staff for green commuting initiatives by their employer, but that there is some doubt that these would be implemented. The results also show that the vast majority of employees feel that they have to drive to work because of the very poor public transport to the Campus. Many participants were aware of how long their journey to work would take by public transport and in many cases this was three to four times the journey time by car, and twice the cost.

It is significant that only at Sky and for those employees who had relocated to Quintiles from their Riccarton site was there a perception that travel to work was a real problem. For all other staff, it was not; parking is available, journey times are short and roads uncongested. It is significant that many staff are able to go home for lunch ("to do the hoovering").

The culture, small size and nature of the operation at the Royal Bank has made the formation of carsharing arrangements much more common here than at the other employers. Smaller units may engender a greater willingness to help other staff members.

At the end of this research project, in February 2000, the Kirkton Campus Green Commuter Forum appears to be defunct. While there are one or two companies with quite pressing transport problems, for many of the others it may not be a crucial issue at this time. Staff recruitment *is* affected by the area's poor accessibility, but some of the companies in the area are downsizing at the moment. The task for the Chamber of Commerce and for the concerned employers in the Campus is to persuade the others that there is a joint problem which is best tackled as a group. However, evidence from the next case study – the Gyle/New Edinburgh Park in west Edinburgh – suggests that the value of such a joint approach can be limited. Therefore, in the Kirkton Campus context, it may be more valuable for the Council and the Chamber to work only with those organisations such as Cadence and Sky that are identified as having a significant transport problem.

5. CHAPTER FIVE: THE GYLE/NEW EDINBURGH PARK

5.1 Introduction

Because of slow progress with the development of the GCP in the Livingston case study, the second Project Steering Group meeting took the decision to use the Gyle/New Edinburgh Park area as a further case study. This was because it was known to the Steering Group as an area with organisations that were already active in Green Commuter Planning, and that some of the large employers located there had already carried out travel surveys and implemented some measures. It was also known that they had formed a Travel Planning Focus Group (TPFG), under the "honest brokerage" of a chair, an environmental specialist with the Edinburgh Chamber of Commerce and Enterprise (ECCE). Her work as GCP co-ordinator for large organisations in Edinburgh is part funded by the City of Edinburgh Council.

5.2 Structure of this chapter

This chapter first provides background information on the situation that obtains at the Gyle/NEP in terms of numbers of employees, site location, transport access and transport problems. It then gives a brief history of the Gyle/NEP Travel Planning Focus Group – its aims and its work so far in attempting to alleviate some of the transport problems in the area. It then reviews the activities of some of the individual employers in the area and presents the results of interviews and focus groups held with employees and staff at these sites (Scottish Equitable in NEP, Safeway at the shopping centre and the Royal Bank of Scotland in the Gyle Industrial area). Finally, it draws some conclusions about the motivations for and scope of the GCP activities in the Gyle/NEP and in particular considers the value of employers working together. It does not, unfortunately, present any "after" travel survey data at any of the participating employers. This is because all were wary of surveying their employees again so recently after the first survey without any perceived improvements having been delivered in the interim.

5.3 Site location

The Gyle Industrial Estate, the Gyle Shopping Centre and the New Edinburgh Park (NEP) business park are three contiguous but functionally separate entities located in the west of Edinburgh adjacent to the A720 City Bypass at its interchange with the A8 at the Gogar roundabout/underpass. The sites are effectively bounded to the north by the Edinburgh-Fife railway, to the south by the Edinburgh-Glasgow line, and to the west by the A720. The shopping centre is located in the northern portion of the area, the Industrial Estate in the southeastern area and NEP lies to the west (see Figure 5.1).

The main access road to the area is South Gyle Broadway which runs northwest-southeast through the area. Particular points of congestion at peak hours are the Gogar Roundabout, the junction of South Gyle Broadway with Edinburgh Park, and the junction of South Gyle Access Rd with Bankhead Drive. The roads in NEP are unadopted and at peak hours Redheugh's Avenue is blocked by a barrier, with cars wishing to travel through the Park let through only one at a time. This may arguably contribute to further congestion on South Gyle Crescent.

The Gyle Centre is a shopping centre with about 2,000 employees. It has also developed into something of a bus hub, with local services along the A8 and A71 into central Edinburgh, and links to Fife and West Lothian. However, it is between 400m and 800m away from many of the

Figure 5.1: The Edinburgh Park/Gyle Area

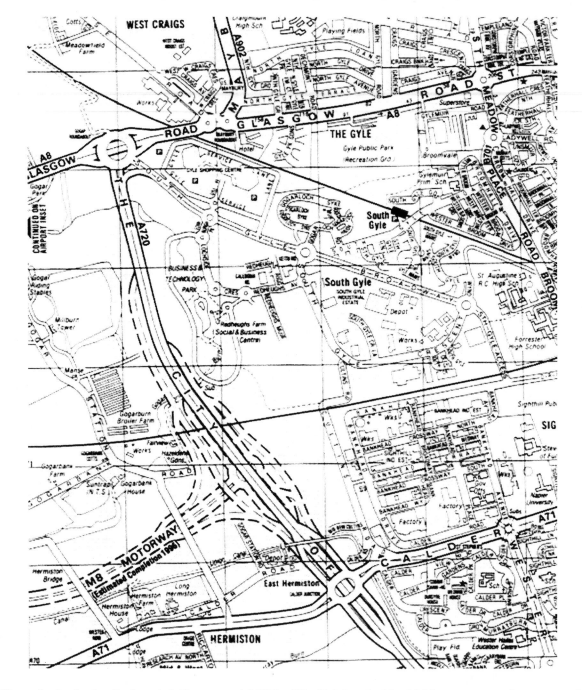

offices in both the Industrial Estate and NEP. Until March 12, 2000, most services ceased at around 20:00. The only bus service running through this area before this date was Lothian Buses 21, on a nominally 12 minute frequency until 1800 when it became half-hourly. Its route took it through the employment area via Redheughs Avenue and Lochside Road. Since this date, however, a major route revision has taken place and the area is now served by a bus to the city centre every 5 minutes (combination of routes 22, 12 and 2), and services run until 2200. The fastest journey time to the city centre is about 20 minutes. The Operations Manager, Lothian Buses, confirmed that lobbying from companies in the area was a significant factor in the decision to upgrade services. Orbital links remain poor, however.

The nearest railway station to the area is South Gyle, approximately 10 minutes' walk from the shopping centre and from the junction of South Gyle Crescent and Redheugh's Avenue. This provides services to the City Centre and to Fife and the northeast. A new station on the Glasgow line, Edinburgh Park, will be built as part of the City of Edinburgh Rapid Transit (CERT), a PFI-funded guided busway from the airport to the City Centre. This is due to be completed in late 2001. While trains to Dunblane and Bathgate will stop at Edinburgh Park, it is still unclear what proportion of the 4 trains per hour to/from Glasgow will call here. CERT will offer a 15 minute journey time from NEP to the City Centre and also a park and ride facility at the airport which may be attractive to those wishing to avoid congestion at Gogar roundabout. (NEP has been permitted to increase its planned parking provision, should CERT not be running by 2002).

South Gyle Industrial Estate has grown up over the past ten years and there are now about 6,000 staff working in the area at employers such as the Bank of Scotland, British Telecom, GEC Marconi, and the Royal Bank of Scotland. It is not possible to put a precise figure on the number of parking spaces available but there is severe parking stress in the area, with cars parked around roundabouts and right into access roads to buildings. There is no management company for the Industrial Estate and the roads are the responsibility of the City of Edinburgh Council.

In contrast, Edinburgh Park has been developed to project a unified image of a "leading edge" business park, rather than simply a collection of buildings in an area. Edinburgh Park Management (EPM) manages the operation of the business park on behalf of the developers (New Edinburgh Ltd.) and the occupiers, each of which pays a service charge. Occupiers buy rather than rent their sites from New Edinburgh Ltd. However, while the site remains in development, the developers and the occupiers - as members of the board of EPM - would have to contribute towards any jointly-agreed transport initiative, such as, for example, subsidised bus services to the area.

Key employers currently on the site are Scottish Equitable, with 2,364 staff (and another 400 moving in); Adobe with 300; British Telecom with 900; and the Midland Bank Call Centre with about 450. The full list of employers in the park is as follows: ICL, BT, Scottish Equitable, UDV, Telewest, HSBC Global Funds, HSBC Call Centre, HQ Business Centre, KSCL, Oracle, FI Group, Halifax, John Menzies and British Energy. A travel survey of all employers has been carried out for the developer but the results remain confidential.

The one common theme that unites NEP, South Gyle and the Gyle Shopping Centre is expansion: NEP is only half built-out; the Shopping Centre has applied for planning permission to increase its floorspace by 30%; and in the industrial estate, new units continue to be built and occupied. Ultimately, it is likely that at least 20,000 employees will be located in the area. It is already the fourth largest concentration of employment in Scotland.

Most of the new developments are now subject to GCP requirements as a planning condition, and parking standards for new buildings are now set as maxima that permit roughly half the employees at a workplace to park on site. In addition, the developers New Edinburgh Limited are now on record as saying that they are seeking to increase the density of the business park by reducing parking standards in subsequent developments. Hence accessibility by modes other than the private car has become central to the overall accessibility level, and ultimately the continued commercial success, of the whole area.

In the Gyle/NEP, in stark contrast to Kirkton Campus, there are more, and more severe, factors that are driving the implementation of green transport measures. It is nonetheless very much the case that it is those employers/developers that are planning expansions, and those with untenable parking problems, that are most active. The peak hour congestion in accessing the area that affects all its occupants is much less of a stimulus to activity in green commuter planning.

5.4 Gyle/NEP Employers Focus Group

An initial meeting of Gyle and Edinburgh Park representatives was called by the Royal Bank of Scotland (RBS) in November 1998. The group was formed and meets 6-weekly. The members of the group are as follows:

David Mathie Ian Fairgrieve	Royal Bank of Scotland
Gordon Paterson	Edinburgh Park Management
Gordon Bell	HBSC
Alan Knott	Scottish Equitable
Gerry McCann Shonagh Jack	Mark & Spencer
Deborah Robertson	Gyle Shopping Centre
John Cannon	Scottish Courage Brewers
Retired – to be replaced	Bank of Scotland
Ian Forrest	Scottish Provident
Michael Somerville	BT
Tom Rye	Napier University
Caryll Paterson (Convenor)	Edinburgh Chamber of Commerce

The Napier University representative was invited to the group because of his knowledge of green commuter planning elsewhere, and to provide research/information support. The aims of the group were to address joint concerns over traffic congestion and parking difficulties, and to share best practice in the development of Company Travel Plans to bring about a reduction in solo occupancy car trips. In order to achieve these aims, the group set five objectives which were subsequently pursued by actions by different members of the group. The most active members of the group, besides the Convener, have been the RBS and Edinburgh Park Management (EPM).

5.5 Group Objectives:

1. To identify common problems and to investigate practical solutions and possible joint initiatives.
2. To increase public transport usage by promoting existing services and by improving service provision.
3. To improve safety conditions for walkers, cyclists and public transport users, and for motorists.
4. To reduce and eliminate dangerous and inconsiderate parking.
5. To raise awareness of Gyle/Edinburgh Park as the 4th largest Commercial centre in Scotland and lobby for appropriate levels of infrastructure.

The actions taken by the group to address each of these objectives are set out below in turn.

5.5.1 Objective 1

Table 5.1: Travel survey results, Gyle/NEP

	Royal Bank		Bank of Scotland		Gyle Centre		Scottish Courage		HSBC		Scottish Equitable		BT		Marks and Spencer		Scottish Provident		Other New Edinburgh Park		TOTAL	
	n	%	n	%	n	%	N	%	n	%	n	%	n	%	n	%	n	%	n	%	n	%
Current employees	1600		1753		100		360		494		2364				380				850		7901	
Projected employees	2500		1800		100		360		700		2500		900		380		100				9340	
Parking spaces (ratio)	1160	.73	674	.38			165	.46	280		1200	.51			70	.18					3549	.45
Responses	1353		823				87				1790				145				504		4702	
Travel survey %		84.5		47				24				76				38				59.2		60%
Response rate																						
Work times																						
Arrive 8 – 9	989	73.1					65	72														
Leave 5 – 6	875	64.7																				
Commute mode																						
solo car	907	67.0	708	86.0			58	66.7			1269	70.9			78	53.8			353	70.0	3373	71.7
Carshare	235	17.4	49	6.0			16	18.4			511	28.5			0	0.0			50	9.9	862	18.3
bus	238	17.6	49	6.0			1	1.1			132	7.4			39	26.9			66	13.1	525	11.2
Train	95	7.0	8	1.0			8	9.2							10	6.9			10	2.0	131	2.8
Alternative modes																						
Consider bus	409	30.2	247	30.0															121	24.0	777	16.5
Consider train/CERT	310	22.9	181	22.0															71	14.1	562	12.0
Consider carshare	860	63.6					40				577										1477	31.4

NB where data are missing from this table, this is because they have not been returned by the companies involved. This information was collated by Edinburgh Chamber of Commerce and Enterprise.

Most group members have or will conduct surveys of staff travel patterns, and details of almost 10,000 personnel have now been collated to show geographic distribution and modal split (see Table 5.1). This information also provides a sample of current employee perceptions and attitudes to the various modes.

It has already been noted, but should be emphasised, that although some "before" travel surveys have been carried out, no "after" surveys have yet been conducted to measure the modal shift impacts of the measures implemented at the Gyle. None of the organisations in the Focus Group was keen to have another survey conducted when there was a general perception that alternative modes of travel had not been put in place. The effects of the RBS carsharing scheme and other GCP measures can, however, be inferred from the fact that their car parking problems have been alleviated. It is difficult to measure accurately but, based on the allocation of carsharing parking permits, it is now likely that somewhere between 30 and 40% of RBS staff carshare to work. Hence it can be concluded that this GCP has had modal shift effects – but in the context of a massive staff relocation and an acute parking situation.

5.5.2 Objective 2 – initiatives to encourage better public transport services

Obviously the promotion and improvement of public transport services is a key part of any GCP, as the chapter on HP has shown. At the Gyle/NEP there have been a number of initiatives to promote bus use, some of which have been successful and others less so. These fall into three main areas: negotiating discounts with operators; lobbying operators for improved services; and funding services directly. Only one employer has directly subsidised a bus for its employees, but only for a limited period (see below). There was some consideration given to joint funding of a bus service but the subsidy required by the operator was considered too high for all employers concerned and so the question of how to share out a joint subsidy never arose. None of the employers on the site makes any contribution to the commuting costs of those employees who travel to work by public transport, with the exception of the interest foregone on season ticket loans.

ECCE negotiated a 10% discount with LRT on their annual season ticket for organisations developing Green Transport Plans. All members of the group were eligible and the discount was offered to employees, on an interest-free loan basis, from March 1999. Take up by Group members' employees now totals 204 (of 1039 Edinburgh-wide). This offer will continue and LRT has agreed to produce new literature to enable the group to re-market the offer. Of the 1039 users across Edinburgh who have taken up the offer, 89 are new customers to Lothian Buses, but their previous mode is not known.

Edinburgh Park Management began negotiations with LRT in early 1999 to improve bus services to the whole Gyle/NEP area. A potential route for a new service was mapped out, based on servicing the greatest demand, and a proposal was presented to LRT. This would have run from the Stockbridge/Comely Bank area (half a mile to the north of Edinburgh City Centre), through Davidson's Mains and Drum Brae to the Gyle and Edinburgh Park. It would have then run on to the western villages of Currie and Balerno. LRT agreed that it could provide the service, but only if costs of £250,000 per year were 100% underwritten by employers in the area. It was decided by members that this would be too costly an exercise and the offer was declined at that time. RBS approached other bus operators over the summer of 1999, to similarly improve services, but these have failed to achieve substantial results.

In August 1999 Neil Renilson, the Chief Executive of LRT, was invited to address the group, to investigate joint activities. He made a strong point that LRT would not be introducing new services to Gyle/Edinburgh Park in the belief that they would be commercially unviable. He suggested that the 21 and 12 were excellent services and proposed to increase the frequency of these to give combined frequency to the city centre of 12 buses per hour, and to extend their duration to 10 pm, from early 2000. He declined to offer peak-hour express services along these routes, on the basis that it would be too costly. However, he voiced an interest in selling a private express bus service to the group as an alternative.

RBS hired a private coach from LRT, which they offered free to their employees for a 12 week period from August of 1999. It ran a peak hour express service (4 departures each way each day) and was extremely popular. However, this was a temporary measure intended to assist staff who had been relocated from city centre sites to the Younger Building, the second phase of RBS' office construction in the Gyle area (it has an option to develop a third site).

RBS opened negotiations with LRT to continue the express service on a commercial basis, open to all personnel in the area. After a number of meetings with the group and RBS, LRT came back with a final offer: to provide a guaranteed-seat commuter service, plus unlimited use of all other Lothian services, for individuals purchasing a £350 annual season ticket (£51 premium on the discounted ticket). The additional cost was because the commuter service, as a private bus, is not eligible for fuel duty rebate. The service was to be offered only upon registration of 83 individuals, but unfortunately only 8 applications were received. It is believed that the cause of failure was the extremely poor promotion and short deadlines demanded by Lothian, and also because there would have been only one bus per day each way until a second group of 83 users had signed up to the idea, when a second service could be offered.

A new LRT service in the area, the number 58, was extended in January to run on from Longstone to serve the Napier University campuses of Craiglockhart, Craighouse and Merchiston. This is subsidised by Napier University at a cost of £1,800 per week for an experimental 13 week period. Again, this subsidy is sufficient to run the service empty, that is, there is no risk taken by the bus operator.

In February 2000 ECCE approached First Group with a view to improving services to the area. There is an initial enthusiasm to improve services to build demand prior to introduction of CERT in 2002, but negotiations have not begun yet. A high-level representative of FirstGroup, speaking at a recent Association of Commuter Transport Conference on Jan 31st in London, voiced the opinion that the potential of initiatives with employers lay in incremental expansions to existing routes where there is a good level of interpeak demand. In general, he does not believe that isolated employment areas are a commercial proposition for bus operators because of the highly peaked but spatially dispersed demand at such locations.

In May 1999 the Commercial Director and Manager for ScotRail addressed the group. They advised of improvements to Gyle Station including installation of safety features. They noted their commitment to linking with CERT at Edinburgh Park Station, though were unable to give a commitment to stop the Glasgow-Edinburgh trains. They were of the view that they would be unable to cope with additional demand on peak services to/from Fife, which are already over-capacity. They presented a Gyle rail publicity and information leaflet, and subsequently agreed to consider the group's suggestion of "early bird" discounts (as introduced on several London commuter lines); as of February 2000, these have not materialised.

The members of the group feel that they have done considerable work to indicate to bus and rail operators the size of the potential public transport travel market at the Gyle/NEP. The response from bus and rail operators is perceived to have been lack lustre at best. While there is a recognition from the Gyle employers that the public transport operators are commercial organisations that must make a profit, it is felt that they are particularly risk averse and unwilling to run services experimentally at a loss. There is a further perception that the public transport operators' marketing of their services is extremely poor, in spite of the fact that the organisations at the Gyle were in effect offering them access to the potential market of 12,000+ employees.

It is unclear to what extent the organisations at the Gyle would be willing to underwrite services themselves, as has been done by organisations such as Boots in Nottingham, Pfizer in Kent, BP Amoco in Sunbury (West London), Stockley Park (also in West London) and Southampton General Hospital and University. It was clear after the initial negotiations with LRT for a new Comely Bank to Balerno service that £250,000 per year was felt to be too much to pay, but further discussions have not clarified how much, if anything at all, *would* be an acceptable amount.

From the point of view of the operators, locations such as the Gyle/NEP are not good bus operating territory, since demand is so highly peaked but so spatially dispersed. In addition, there is much more parking available than would be found in a city centre with a comparable number of jobs, giving a major incentive to staff to take their cars to work. However, the Gyle area does have the advantage compared to a location such as Kirkton Campus that there is the shopping centre to provide at least some base level of interpeak demand. Nonetheless, this would be at a level much below that of a city centre because, once again, there is ample free parking, and trips to the centre are complex and dispersed.

5.5.3 Objectives 3 and 4 - to improve conditions for cyclists and walkers, and to eliminate dangerous and inconsiderate parking

A key problem in the Gyle area is inconsiderate parking and rat running. At peak hours drivers rat run through the shopping centre in order to avoid queues on the Broadway. In addition there is anecdotal evidence that employees from the Gyle/NEP are parking all day in the shopping centre car park, in spite of a nominal time limit. During the day, South Gyle Crescent is completely parked up, causing particular problems for pedestrians and buses. Finally there is a perception that traffic speeds on South Gyle Broadway (a dual carriageway with a 40 mph limit) are so high that they are a deterrent to pedestrians wishing to cross – although two pelican crossings and a subway are provided.

It should be noted that, as the roads in NEP are privately owned, on-street parking is adequately enforced and rat running can be prevented by use of the barrier on Redheughs Drive.

In an attempt to solve the problems in the Gyle, the group invited the City of Edinburgh Council and the Police service to address the group at its July 1999 meeting. A number of safety concerns were highlighted and the group appealed for solutions. The group drew attention to dangerous and fugitive parking, and observed that there was no policing of this area. The Police were of the view that they were unable to assist, however, because of priorities elsewhere.

The Council officials present offered assurances that some yellow lining of had been approved and was to be implemented. The Council noted that a current (1999/2000) feasibility study will investigate the extension of controlled parking zones (CPZs) to this area. This would improve policing of dangerous parking. A more detailed response to the issues raised by the Council was received by the group at its October meeting. A summary of the response is as follows:

- In general, requests for capacity enhancements to road infrastructure will not be entertained as this runs against general Council policy and would be likely to induce new trips.
- Much emphasis was put by Council officers on CERT's potential to reduce peak hour traffic in the area and encourage modal shift. Members of the group were sceptical of this argument and believe that the number of car parking spaces is a more realistic determinant of the mode split for the area.
- The Council officers also noted the Council's extremely limited budget for traffic management and road safety schemes, but indicated that funding contributions through planning agreements would be welcome.
- Congestion in the area is highly peaked and although there may be considerable numbers of damage-only accidents, the very short period each day when there are large numbers of drivers and pedestrians on the road results in a very low injury accident rate. This is what drives the allocation of the Council's road safety resources and under this policy the Gyle area is a low priority.
- Parking around the Gyle Crescent/Redheugh's Avenue roundabout would be addressed with the application of double yellow lines. As of February 2000, these are not yet in place.
- Parking across dropped kerbs and around entrances to premises would be addressed with the application of non-enforcible white lines. As of February 2000, these too are not yet in place.

As with the bus operators, there was some frustration expressed by group members that the Council were not able or willing to do more to alleviate perceived problems in the area. Members were of the opinion that development had been encouraged in the Gyle/NEP area without the necessary prior investment in transport infrastructure to carry the trips generated.

5.6 Activities of selected companies

The following represents a sample of activities by individual employers. These employers have been selected for a number of reasons:
- firstly, because they represent a range of employers in the area;
- secondly, to give a spread between NEP and the Gyle;
- thirdly, because it was important to include in the sample those employers that have been active; and
- finally, and pragmatically, because these were the employers who were available for interviews and/or focus groups.

5.6.1 Royal Bank of Scotland

Much of the following information is based on interviews with the Project Manager, Central Support, Property and Facilities Department of the Royal Bank, and with the Royal Bank's Environmental Manager. These took place on 22/11/99 and 10/1/00 respectively.

The Royal Bank offices at the Gyle carry out many of the Head Office functions of the organisation. There is a call centre, a retail branch, a cash handling operation, and many other different operational units. Working hours within different functional units are a reflection of business requirements; flexitime is permitted where it can be accommodated without negative impacts on the business.

While the Royal Bank has been a key member of the Edinburgh Travel Planning Focus Group from an early stage, and the Environmental Manager had for some time been warning about the access and congestion problems that the Gyle/NEP area is facing, the catalyst for the Bank's GCP really came when 900 staff relocated to a new building (the Younger Building) from City Centre sites, in July 1999. The Younger Building brought together with the existing Drummond House brings a combined total of 2500 staff on the site during normal business hours; however, for these staff, there are only 1163 parking spaces. RBS was therefore faced with the need to somehow manage parking and so implemented GCP measures. These measures are as follows.

- Provision of cycle racks and shower facilities for staff
- Regular communications to staff by way of "Travel Update" bulletins
- RBS was instrumental in establishing South Gyle Travel Forum with active participation maintained since inception
- Sharing of objectives and information with neighbouring businesses
- Extensive staff travel surveys were carried out
- A database was created with details of staff and their travel to work patterns, based on the travel survey.
- A policy and prioritisation scheme for parking space allocation and car park management was implemented.
- A carsharing scheme was introduced, run through the Bank's Intranet (over 40% of parking spaces were reserved for sharers).
- Bus and Rail companies were lobbied for improved services
- Local Authority and Police were lobbied for improved traffic control and pedestrian safety measures
- A free bus was provided between the City Centre and South Gyle for six months to encourage staff to use communal transport. A travel club option was developed to replace the free bus but this proved too expensive and impractical for the majority of staff at the Gyle. This option was hurriedly pulled together as a an alternative to the withdrawn free bus service and it was not possible in the time available to fully research and market the idea throughout the Gyle site at the time.
- A "roadshow" by the Council's public transport Traveline information service was facilitated in staff restaurant, and a dedicated staff travel noticeboard set up
- Details of bus and rail company offers were advised to staff

- Flexible working was introduced where business operations permit

The most contentious of these measures by far was the carsharing scheme; essentially, for staff who are not Executives, Senior Management, essential business users (verified by senior managers), or those working unsocial hours, no parking space would be provided unless staff were in a carsharing arrangement with at least one fellow member of staff. Some 2242 applications were received for parking spaces, and 1862 people received a parking permit, with spaces were allocated as follows:

- Executives and Senior Managers – 118 reserved spaces
- Essential business users – 264 spaces
- Those on unsocial hours, registered and disabled – 186 spaces
- Remaining 480 spaces allocated to carsharers with at least 2 people in a carshare team (in total 1079 staff). Each team is allocated one parking permit per person so they can rotate the use of cars. The partnership is allowed to park in a designated row in the car park and so if two cars with the same permit are parked in that row, the staff in question are contacted. There is random enforcement by security staff who were already on site (i.e. enforcement is not a new or additional cost).
- Spaces for visitors must be booked in advance and are limited in number.

Staff can register to form a carshare through the Bank's intranet, using GIS-linked database software designed in house by one software engineer in 10 days. Setting up the scheme overall took two person months of the Project Manager's time and 3 person weeks of that of his boss. In addition, to carry out the staff travel survey and to collate and evaluate data, there was a £10,000 internal consultancy charge.

Enforcement purges take place every one to two months. The most recent weeded out bogus carshare teams – someone from Falkirk sharing with someone from South Gyle Crescent, for example. At these times, the administration of the carshare scheme takes up to 60% of one administrator's time. At other times, it is no more than 10% of their time.

The Project Manager identified that a key element in the implementation of the scheme was to get senior management (Executive) support for the programme. This was gained in three stages. Firstly, the Director of Property and Facilities presented an initial awareness raising paper to the Executive. A subsequent paper set out the case for preparatory data gathering. A final paper presented data and options for schemes to manage the car parking problem; the recommended option, of the carsharing scheme, was accepted and the resources released to put it into effect.

Information about the travel survey and then the carsharing/parking allocation scheme was handled by Property and Facilities. It was passed out to designated Department co-ordinators at a senior level, who were then responsible for cascading it to staff within their business area. Given that parking is seen by most as a reasonably critical operational issue, there was a willingness throughout the organisation to support the process. Nonetheless both Department co-ordinators and the Property and Facilities Department received many difficult phone calls and emails during the run-up to the introduction of the scheme and for a couple of weeks thereafter.

Essentially, RBS has solved its acute car parking problem on its own through the introduction of a sophisticated carsharing database. The Project Manager felt that more costly or interventionist measures, such as continuing subsidies for company buses, or parking charges, would not be acceptable to the Executive because of cost, manageability and/or industrial relations implications, given the UK context of the RBS operation.

The RBS has been one of the most active organisations in the Gyle/NEP Travel Planning Focus Group. The Property Manager's perception of this group was that, although there were many company representatives willing to attend the group, there were few who were willing to actually take on work associated with it, to "stand up and be counted". There was a need within the group to identify pieces of work and to allocate it on a cross-company basis; without this sharing of activities – which to a large extent has not happened – then the more active members may well start asking themselves whether or not it is worth their while to spend much time working to benefit other local companies.

Regarding the group's negotiations with the public transport operators, the Project Manager commented,

> "I see where they're [the public transport operators] are coming from – but our political decision makers need to be made aware that these are real stumbling blocks. There is only so much that individual companies can do on their own – we need assistance from government. A greater commercial focus from transport providers is required to develop a new customer base rather than simply providing better facilities for existing travellers."

This comment has relevance both to individual organisations and to groups of employers trying to work together.

5.6.2 Royal Bank of Scotland Focus Group

A second strand of the research at the Royal Bank was the use of a focus group of staff to give their feedback on the quality and effectiveness of, and the justification for, the Bank's GCP measures. Some eighteen staff were recruited, of whom some nine turned up. Two are bus users, one walks, one takes the train and the others carshare. A sample of the focus group schedule used in the Gyle is illustrated in Appendix 5.1.

The schedule for the focus group was similar to that used at Scottish Equitable and Safeway (appended). It asked employees how they currently get to work, what problems they experience on their commute, how much easier it would be to use "greener" modes (if applicable), and what and whether their employer might consider assisting them in so doing. In this group, as in others, it was explained that the focus of the group should be on measures that the organisation (or groups of adjacent employers together) could implement to assist employees in their commute and to make the commute "greener"; nonetheless, in all groups, discussion constantly drifted towards issues that were *external* to the organisation. These included the quality of the local road network, congestion on the bypass, the inadequacy of local bus services (in terms of early and late buses, the density of the network or the journey times), and the reliability of local train services from Fife. There were always many more suggestions as to how these elements could be improved than ideas about the role that the organisation should play in combating traffic problems.

The key problems for those commuting to the Royal Bank depend on their mode. For car users, principal problems revolved around travel along the City Bypass and through Gogar Roundabout and access to and especially from the car park to the bypass. *"Getting out of this bloody car park is murder"* was a typical comment. The growth in traffic on the bypass was noted by many, as were the problems with inconsiderate parking and rat running through the shopping centre. As one participant noted,

> *"At nine o'clock [am] I'm one and a quarter hours from Musselburgh. I've had two crashes. The lorries, the cars and everything. It took one and a half hours by bus. Wallyford Station is five minutes from my house - problems - so all-in-all you're harassed".*

Regarding bus travel, staff had equally vehement complaints, such *as "Cramond's crap for buses"*, and this slightly more lucid comment about certain Lothian services:

> *"The problem with the number 21 [LRT] is that it finishes at six-thirty so I go up the road for a number 12 [LRT] on my own in the dark. Three-quarters of an hour to one hour it takes me - the bus service absolutely stinks - it should be extended."*

The general absence of orbital services was identified as a key problem, especially for those living in MidLothian.

Infrastructure problems were also noted. These include the barrier across Redheugh's Avenue and the queues that form at the junction of Lochside with South Gyle Broadway. Several staff felt there was a need for a third exit from the area directly into the Hermiston Gait junction (M8/A720); and that more parking should be provided. As one staff member said, *"The Royal Bank has a lot of clout – how about a multistorey car park?"* Another suggested that the Bank should pay NEP to allow staff through Redheugh's Ave without the barrier.

The Royal Bank is unusual in that it has implemented some significant GCP measures, so staff were asked to comment on these. There was some disquiet that the company had discontinued the free bus service to the City Centre, but there were more perceived problems with the carsharing scheme. In particular, it was perceived to impose inflexibility upon staff. Problems arise when staff need to work late or, as happened on the day of the focus group, weather conditions result in one member of a carshare arrangement being unable to get to the rendezvous point. There was also a perception that the car park was not always full and that some carshare arrangements were less genuine and more simply a ruse to get around the regulations. The most important additional measure that the Bank could provide was to allow more flexitime working, so that peaks are staggered. As one participant said, *"staggered times would make so much of a difference"*.

An overwhelming feeling came out of this and the other Gyle focus groups that the area was built in the wrong place and that local and national government had neither planned nor invested in the infrastructure sufficiently, nor set up a public transport system that could cope with the travel demand generated at out of town sites.

> *"God forsaken hole put here - you get the smell of the chicken factory over there...Edinburgh does not have the capacity to deal with all this development..."*

For those who had previously worked in the city centre, there was a general dislike of these sites as well – as one person said, in reference to relocation, *"I don't think it should take any longer to get here than it did in town."* There was a recognition of the much better public transport accessibility of the city centre sites.

In summary, it would appear that the average Royal Bank commuter has a grudging acceptance of the Bank's carsharing scheme. She or he finds the location of the Bank difficult to reach by any mode of transport because of congestion, unreliability and lack of parking. Few GCP measures are identified; in contrast, considerable responsibility is laid at the door of government and public transport operators to improve both the planning and the service to such locations – and to think twice about developing such areas in future.

5.7 Safeway Focus Group

Safeway supermarket is located in the Gyle Shopping Centre and employs 450 staff on a wide variety of shifts and weekly working hours. It was felt important to conduct a focus group in a retail employer because of these different working patterns and also because of the lower wages that generally obtain in such organisations compared to the financial employers across the road. Nonetheless, many similar issues arose here as at the RBS and Scottish Equitable; indeed the only problem that was *not* identified at Safeway was employee parking.

Seven staff attended the focus group: one rail user, two bus users, one carsharer/bus user, and three drivers. While five of the attendees live reasonably locally, the other two (both drivers) live in Lanarkshire and commute by car. They agreed that it would in theory be possible for them to carshare but that varying shift times make it difficult in practice.

Key transport problems were the lack of out of hours public transport, and congestion. Key comments included the following:

> *"The bus can be impossible and unrealistic when it's late. It's a 45 minute walk [from Wester Hailes] but I'm put off doing it because you can get followed. The bus is unrealistic."*

> *"It's the same for me [i.e. having to take two buses] - I live 4 miles away at Davidson's Mains - I had to get two buses and it was a tight schedule. I've now got a car and I use it. I'd take the bus if it was easier."*

Some explanation for this was offered:

> *"It's mainly profit - privatisation - that they think about. It's standing all the way sometimes and after 6.30 it stops if it's not making money [ref buses]."*

One participant, living in South Queensferry (4 miles to the northwest), was concerned because the bus she depends on to get to work is about to be withdrawn. She risks social exclusion – through potential unemployment - if the train is too expensive or runs at inconvenient times (although incidentally she is able to take advantage of the reduced rail season ticket prices negotiated by Hewlett Packard).

> *"It's unfair that they take the bus off. It's because it's losing money but it's not really been marketed properly. They haven't really let people know that it's stopping. Taking the #456 to Kirkliston and a #38 to South Gyle is the only way I'll be able to get here – but who knows how long that will take?"*

> *"If there was no train service to South Queensferry to fall back on I couldn't work here. I'd be unemployed if I had to work in South Queensferry [regular bus user]."*

For those driving from further away, there are other problems.

> *"The M8's a car park at 8.30 - forget it. If it's a 6.30 start OK - 9.00 you can be lucky. I'd a 9.00 start - I left at 7.05 [from Motherwell] and arrived 9.15 - an hour to get through Gogar."*

One of the car drivers, a manager, helps people to get to and from work, particularly at unsocial hours, by giving them lifts and going out of his way to do so. As he said, *"this adds time to my day"*, but without him so doing, staff could not get to and from work at the times demanded by the business. This point was expanded on by one other member of the group, who felt that because of these (often unsocial) hours required by the company, it really had a responsibility to get involved in helping people get to and from work. But she recognised, firstly, that

> *"There are too many different shifts for the company to run work buses. It could work if core times were similar. Company minibuses could run from Davidson's Mains and Wester Hailes"*

and also that recruitment – although a problem – was not yet sufficient of a problem for the company to take such interventionist action, and to spend money. Another member of the group agreed that the company should get involved, but another countered that, *"When you took the job you knew the score - it's not really the company's problem."*

Besides works buses, the only other GCP initiative that the participants felt that Safeway could pursue was cycle facilities – particularly parking and showers – although it was also noted that this would only appeal to a minority of mostly male staff.

5.8 Scottish Equitable Focus Groups

The green travel initiatives at Scottish Equitable have been to take part in the Travel Planning Focus Group meetings, to promote carsharing (via email and noticeboards, but not through a formal system such as the one at the Royal Bank) and to promote the LRT offer(s). Whilst its parking structure is at capacity, there is an overspill car park ten minutes to the west that is rarely full. However, the organisation is growing rapidly and it is also likely that the overspill car park will be redeveloped, so Scottish Equitable's transport problems will become more acute.

Two focus groups took place at Scottish Equitable, both in December 1999. Some nine staff attended in all: one carsharer, one train user, three bus users and four lone drivers. Of the commuting problems experienced, parking and access to and from the bypass were again significant for the car drivers; unreliable train services from Fife were key for the rail user; and slow and unreliable services, particularly from the east of Edinburgh, were key for the bus users. This participant was typical, in that she experiences traffic problems, but also recognises the contribution that her and her fellow commuters make to these problems:

> "The only problem is Gogar Roundabout. On an average day I can get [parked] close but it can take half an hour to park. Scottish Equitable puts an extra fifteen hundred cars on the road [each day] - other companies are doing the same."

There was a range of feeling on whether the company should and would implement a GCP. Some felt that there was an argument for it:

> "[In] some ways not really - it's up to the individual but I think if people could get into work by train and bus easily you'd have less stressed out people and fewer accidents. It took [colleague's name] three hours to get into work - it's not healthy."

and another argued that

> "One problem is recruiting and keeping experienced staff. The company would lose out on a retention basis."

However, others felt that the responsibility was not wholly that of the company:

> "It's not up to Scottish Equitable; it's up to LRT and the Scottish Executive to do this."

> "There's a three-way responsibility: company, local government and government."

Some feedback was given on the GCP initiatives which have been taken by Scottish Equitable. In general, these were perceived to be half-hearted and not particularly effective. As one participant noted with regard to the carsharing scheme,

> "You can have a look at the Car Share Bulletin Board - mostly folk without cars put their name down."

Some years ago the company ran shuttle buses to and from the city centre (shortly after it relocated to NEP), but these were discontinued. This was cited as an example of the company being unlikely to devote large resources to a GCP. As another participant commented,

"Yes, they (Scottish Equitable] have tried but the minute it hits the [Scottish Equitable] pocket it's not on. If it's going to cost, they're not interested."

and another commented that *"the problems are just being kept at bay".*

Many additional possible GCP measures were however suggested. These included an NEP-wide carsharing scheme (now to be implemented); preferential reserved parking spaces for carsharers; compressed working weeks; and teleworking (although some people were concerned about the costs of a modem link from home). One participant also suggested that Scottish Equitable could move back into the city centre.

This relates to perhaps the strongest feeling from both Scottish Equitable groups: that the office was in the wrong place and that transport infrastructure and services had failed to keep pace with the scale of the development. This was perceived to be partly a failure of planning and partly a failure of public transport deregulation and privatisation. The following comments sum up these perceptions very well:

"Edinburgh Park are boasting about getting thousands in but the infrastructure is just not up to it."

"Three and a half years now but it's all empty promises - it's a victim of its own success - more staff than we ever thought."

"Edinburgh Park should not have been opened here."

Overall, the impression from the focus groups is that travel to work at the Gyle/NEP is perceived as something of a struggle. At some workplaces, employees see that their employers could implement measures to make the commute easier and/or greener for staff, but that the problems are not presently causing such operational difficulties that, with the exception of the Royal Bank, significant resources will be invested to alleviate them. All focus groups felt that the responsibility for solving transport problems lies in part with employers but much more with the central and local government in both planning and then servicing such new development areas.

5.9 HSBC Midland Bank

Much of the information in this section of the report is based on an interview with Gordon Bell, Operations Manager, 13th January 1999. The business is a bank; this call centre is one of four Customer Service Centres (CSCs) (the others are located in Swansea, Leeds and Hemel Hempstead; calls are automatically routed to whichever call centre has had an operator off the phone for the longest period). The Operations Manager stressed that his CSC is purely a cost to HSBC, rather than actually generating business. He was also at pains to suggest that the CSCs had a different, more "people-centred" culture to the bank as a whole.

One of the attractions of the location was that it was to be well served by public transport. Edinburgh Park is supposed to have its own station on the Glasgow-Edinburgh line, and the City of Edinburgh Rapid Transit (CERT) guided bus scheme is planned to run right past the CSC. However, at the soonest, these infrastructure improvements will come on stream in 2002 and 2001 respectively. Hence the CSC is left with something of an accessibility and parking problem.

In January 1999, the call centre staff consisted of 410 telephone operators and 50 managers and admin workers. However, it is growing, and by the end of 1999 some 580 people worked there. Staff turnover is not a problem at present although some 150 of staff have moved on by that date since the centre opened.

The centre is open 0800-2200 Monday to Friday, 0800-1900 Saturday, and 1000-1900 on Sunday. There are definite peak days (Monday and Friday), and peaks within the day (lunchtime and early evening). However, staff work regular, predictable shifts and are not required to be "on call" at home, ready to come in to work if demand warrants it. Staff can, in negotiation with management, choose their preferred shift. Main shifts are 0800-1400 and 1200-2000 on weekdays. Thus parking demand is at its maximum during lunch hours, especially on Mondays and Fridays.

The banking union BIFU is recognised at this workplace but Mr Bell was not specific as to the number of employees who are members. Two employees - site manager and one other - qualify for company cars. There is very little travel on works' business, because of the nature of the operation.

The building has 200 car parking spaces. Access to these spaces is not controlled. In addition, the CSC has recently begun renting a further 80 adjacent spaces, 40 from British Energy (access controlled by swipe card) and 40 from John Menzies. This costs £500/space/year (£40,000). Obtaining permission from head office for this expenditure was not a problem according to the Operations Manager. The additional parking spaces are not fully used at present, but it was necessary to rent them in late 1998 as they might not have been available at a later date - there was competition for them. With these 280 spaces, maximum demand started to outstrip supply in February 1999. Some of the parkers in the CSC car park are from other nearby employers (e.g. Royal Bank of Scotland in the adjacent Gyle Business Park).

A staff travel survey has been conducted. While the Operations Manager did not provide full details, it appears that some 70% of staff currently drive to work. At least sixty drivers share with at least one other person. There is a considerable concentration of staff in the Livingston area.

The motivation for the green transport measures which the CSC is implementing is threefold:

1. Parking problems (current and anticipated).
2. A "green transport intention" related to the culture of the CSC as a "people-centred" place.
3. Poor public transport access which effectively reduces the labour pool from which the call centre can draw.

It is not the case that the CSC has a fully developed GCP for the site. Instead they have implemented some measures (marked with an asterisk) and are considering others. These are as follows:

- Installation (and subsequent upgrade) of a bicycle rack *
- Installation of showers*
- Two full staff travel surveys*
- Development and maintenance of a database of staff postcodes and working patterns to encourage carsharing*
- Promotion of certain work patterns with travel outside peak times*
- Priority spaces in the car park for carsharers and motor cycle users*
- Interest free season ticket loans*
- Bus/rail information displayed, and visits by Traveline representatives from the Council*
- When the NEP carsharing database comes on line HSBC staff will have access to it.
- The CSC is also considering providing a works bus service, probably from the Livingston area.

HSBC's problems are not as severe as those at RBS, but severe enough for them to implement certain measures. These have largely been independent of the Gyle Group, although HSBC have been regular attendees.

5.10 Edinburgh Park (Management) on behalf of its member organisations

EP(M)L is currently installing an intranet system which will be available to all the above companies directly onto the individual employee's desk (6000+). This will provide amongst others a comprehensive green transport policy to include:
- Car sharing either within each company or company wide. This will be initially the companies located at Edinburgh Park with potential expansion capabilities to include the greater Gyle area.
- Comprehensive details of public transport arriving and departing within the surrounding area to include CERT, rail and air.
- It is hoped that this will become real time when made available by the public transport providers.
- When available real time road traffic conditions in and around the area.
- Details of other modes of transportation eg cycling, walking, taxis and car pools with information on clubs or co-operatives and maps of routes to and from the local area.
- On-Line workplace shopping (depending on the local retail organisations).

In addition EP(M)L operate a strict no additional parking policy, actively promote new and enhanced public transport to and from the local area, are currently seeking to make Edinburgh Park more pedestrian friendly with the possible introduction of pedestrian crossings being considered and by limiting car/vehicle speeds to 20 mph.

A number of barriers were identified. Principally, the bottom-line cost of green commuting measures would have to be justified to the developer and the occupiers. It would be easier to do this if employers outwith the Park were also prepared to contribute to the cost of a plan.

Secondly, the cost of public transport fares and timings of services were identified as operational barriers which would be difficult to solve without changes to the more institutional barrier of lack of public control over public transport services.

5.11 Conclusions to Chapter on Gyle/New Edinburgh Park

The employers in the Gyle/NEP have been meeting together and to an extent working together on green travel issues for some 18 months. They have achieved a number of things: the collection of travel data, the negotiation of a discount with the major bus operator, and considerable lobbying of public transport operators and the local authority. However, it is not clear that these efforts have resulted in many actual improvements or changes in the way in which people get to work. The majority of the members of the group have been willing to attend meetings and to add their voice to the requests to Council and transport operators to improve services and infrastructure.

In terms of actual activities within their own operations, Edinburgh Park Management, the Royal Bank and HSBC (formerly Midland) Bank have been particularly active. They each have their own particular reasons and motivations for these activities, such as planning pressures, lack of parking, relocation and/or recruitment of staff. Other organisations have expended some limited effort on the promotion of carsharing and of LRT ticket offers. Where problems have been alleviated – for example, at the Bank of Scotland, which was given planning permission for a temporary car park – attendance at the group has been less regular than previously. At no time has the group jointly funded any measures, although it is likely that there will be joint funding of a Gyle public transport information booklet (total cost approximately £3,000). There has been no move to set up a Gyle/NEP wide carsharing database, although one is now being developed by EPM Ltd to run in NEP alone, initially.

As noted above, Lothian Buses have in early 2000 very significantly improved their services to the Gyle. It is likely that this is at least partly in response to lobbying from the employers and the shopping centre and so in this sense the group has had an important and positive effect on green transport provision in the area.

The evidence from the Gyle/NEP that GCPs actually work in achieving a modal shift away from the private car is at present limited to the Royal Bank. Although no after survey has been carried out, it is obvious that a significantly greater proportion of the new total number of staff now carshares to work than did so prior to the introduction of the new parking regime. However, this has been achieved by the RBS working on its own and would have been achieved, whether or not the Travel Planning Focus Group had existed.

Thus, it appears from this case study that the benefits of organisations working jointly on transport issues are limited. They can present a united front and a larger market to public transport operators who will at least sit up and take notice. They can also give each other mutual support. However, the organisations that are most active are those with the most pressing individual reasons for pursuing GCP measures.

5.11.1 Relationship to model of GCP development

The Gyle/NEP area's organisations are distributed along the continuum of stages in this model. However, the formation of the Travel Planning Focus Group has had the effect of skewing the average position towards the contemplation/preparation/action stages. RBS is at the maintenance stage of the model but at the same time continues to pursue improved public transport, so in this sense is also in the action stage. The action stage can also be divided according to the degrees of activity undertaken by organisations. Finally, at least one organisation has suffered relapse.

5.11.2 Promoting joint working

There is an obvious and important contrast between NEP and the Gyle in their approach to GCP initiatives. In the former area the management company has a remit to pursue infrastructure and transport initiatives on behalf of the developer and occupiers as part of the overall management of the park. There is no equivalent manager for the Gyle. This suggests that there may be a role for a transportation management association, on the American model, to replicate the activities of EPM over the wider Gyle area. This would be an ideal area for further policy-relevant applied research.

Both employees and those staff more intimately involved in the GCP work at the Gyle/NEP have identified some institutional barriers to GCPs: the cost and quality of public transport; the location of employment in areas such as these; and the failure to build adequate transport infrastructure at the time the business park or industrial area is opened.

6. CHAPTER SIX: CONCLUSIONS AND FURTHER WORK

6.1 Model of GCP development

The reader will recall the model of GCP development presented in Chapter One, which can better help us to understand the development of GCPs in the case studies in this project. The stages are:

- Pre-contemplation
- Contemplation
- Preparation
- Action, further divided into:
  - *Basic*
  - *Incentives*
  - *Disincentives*
- Maintenance
- Relapse

It is clear that Hewlett Packard has reached the stage of action with incentives, and is now maintaining its plan. The maintenance of the plan depends on continuing management support which the interviews and the analysis of HP's corporate culture suggest will both be forthcoming in the medium term. The interviews do indicate that the EHS Manager has been a key figure in the implementation and now maintenance of the plan, but that he is not without others to support him. It is probable that, even if he were to leave, the plan in its current state would continue. However, both the addition of more incentives, or a shift of the plan into the *disincentives* stage of the model, appear to be unlikely at this stage. Possible potential catalysts for this include further parking stress caused by a very large increase in the number of employees, or changes in government policy, particularly with regard to a PNR (private non-residential) parking levy, which could be levied by local authorities. If the plan does not develop with the addition of further incentives and disincentives, then the panel survey data and evidence from the literature (e.g. Schreffler, 1996) indicates that the overall effect on employee modal split is likely to be in the range 5-8%. The comparison of 1997 and 1999 travel survey data show that a change within this range has indeed been achieved. This importance of this result should not be underestimated, particularly since HP is one of the first employers in the UK to have monitored the effectiveness of its GCP and shown that it can indeed produce results in the UK context.

At Kirkton Campus the situation is rather different. While a few employers have made some attempts to organise carsharing or lift-giving, the majority are either at the pre-contemplation or contemplation stage of the model. Their precise position depends upon the level of access or parking problem from which they suffer, and also upon the personal interests and awareness of key members of staff, particularly in Facilities and Personnel. Hence for example BSkyB, with the largest number of employees of any employer on the Campus and with a pressing parking problem, is very much at the contemplation stage, while smaller employers may have been in pre-contemplation, at least until they received a letter and/or met with BICS. It seems that the formation of the Commuter Forum under the "honest brokerage" of the Chamber of Commerce has not been a sufficient catalyst to move the employers *as a group* into the action stage. Those companies with the most pressing problems may simply have to work on their own.

At the Gyle, the Royal Bank of Scotland has, like HP, shown that GCPs can work. The formation of the Commuter Forum at the Gyle/NEP has moved most employers from the pre-contemplation stage of the model. If attendance at group meetings and promotion of bus ticket offers can be described as "action", then most are now at the action stage. Nonetheless, for most, this action is quite limited. It is only those employers and organisations subject to planning or parking pressures where action has been concerted to implement a GCP.

6.2 Relating conclusions to project objectives

As noted in Chapter One, the objectives of this study are to:

- Examine the potential and actual contribution of GCPs to achieving modal shift
- To identify the factors which make GCPs successful
- To determine the most effective elements of GCPs
- To identify barriers to GCP implementation, and ways to overcome these

6.3 Achieving modal shift

The results from HP and from the Royal Bank show that GCPs *can* make a contribution to achieving modal shift for commuting away from the private car. In that these GCPs also include the promotion and awareness raising of alternative modes, they may help to reduce car dependence, as staff who previously drove to work find that the alternatives are not as bad as they first expected. There is one HP employee who, as a result of the ScotRail ticket offer, was able to sell his car. This will obviously result in a change in his mode of travel for other journeys. From the attitudinal work generally, however, there is no evidence that other staff who changed mode were doing so for trips other than their commute.

There is a much wider question that has not been addressed by this study: even if GCPs do result in modal shift, does this mean that they will reduce congestion? This question lies outwith the scope of this study but it is a vital one for further research. On individual sites, access roads and within car parks it makes intuitive sense that GCPs will reduce congestion. At the wider network level, in a situation of suppressed demand (e.g. West Edinburgh), this is much more of a moot point and one which should be tested by variable trip matrix modelling. South Gyle Broadway, for example, is a through route into Edinburgh from the west and so, even if the Gyle and NEP employers halved their vehicle trip generation with GCPs, peak capacity on the road might well soon be refilled with drivers travelling to other destinations. At the very local level, then, GCPs can have an effect on parking and congestion, but it is unclear that this is the case at the wider level.

6.4 Factors making GCPs successful and barriers to their success

In answering this question, it is impossible to ignore the reasons for implementing a GCP. Time and again evidence in this study, and in others, shows the importance of a pressing operational problem as the prime motivating factor. This may be parking shortages (RBS/HP), on-site congestion (Boots, Nottingham), planning conditions/objectives (Edinburgh Park), or recruitment/retention (HSBC). General congestion, even at the very local level, appears, from the evidence of the two GCP Focus Groups presented here, to be less of an issue.

Consequently, the lack of a problem is perhaps the single biggest barrier to active GCP implementation. From a policy point of view, therefore, the Government must decide whether it wishes to "create such conditions". In new development it appears to already be doing so – the draft PPG13 puts great emphasis on GCPs, for example. The PNR parking levy is of considerable concern to the businesses and employees who participated in this study, and it could be a means to create the motivation for GCPs in organisations that are not applying for planning permission. However, the PNR levy will not be implemented nationally and so at the national level this tool is not available.

The study of HP has shown the importance of a corporate culture that is conducive to GCP development. HP's GCP fits without difficulty into its existing Health and Safety, Environmental Management and employee welfare programmes. Staff were available to work on the GCP, at periods almost full-time, but this might not have been the case in an organisation where Health and Safety is not so core to the corporate culture. This culture is also key to management support, a further potential barrier.

At the Royal Bank and at HP, management support for measures was gained by a carefully planned three step programme: making a case for a GCP in principle, then gathering data, and then, based on this data, evaluating options for action and gaining approval for these. This essentially technocratic procedure will work in certain types of organisations but in others that are more political, a further stage to the process will be building organisational support prior to gaining management approval. For a fuller discussion of barriers in these (generally more public sector) organisations, the reader is referred to Rye (1997).

Some of the barriers to GCP implementation which are relevant to the case studies are as follows:

- The "organisational peripherality" of GCPs - they are new, and not part of everyday business activity.
- The difficulty of identifying the costs and benefits of GCPs.
- Lack of management support for GCPs.
- A perception among employees that the alternatives to driving do not offer an equivalent level of service.

At HP in particular, many of these barriers have been addressed. The first and third have been overcome by gaining management acceptance that the GCP not only addresses operational concerns, but also fits into HP's culture of providing a good environment for its workforce and in being seen to care for the local and global community. It remains to be seen if the second bullet point will become an issue at HP if the plan develops further. Finally, HP has done a great deal to try to overcome the final barrier by delivering concrete improvements in cycle facilities, a significant decrease in train fares, and by publicising these changes very effectively.

6.5 The effectiveness of different measures

While there is considerable data in the Appendix 3.6 reviewing the importance of different measures at HP, the key measures that appear to have resulted in mode shift are the rail discount at HP and carsharing *combined with parking management* at the Royal Bank. The rail discount is significant at HP but perhaps, even more importantly, the site is located directly adjacent to the station. Thus the benefits of this measure are relatively obvious and it is highly convenient to use (overcrowding and unreliability notwithstanding). Thus there are site-specific aspects to this measure.

It is interesting that at HP levels of carsharing have declined since 1997 in spite of its promotion of this mode (for 3+ carpools). Employees also rate it as a relatively ineffective measure. In contrast, it is the lynchpin of RBS' plan. However, it is effective because it is combined with a disincentive: no carshare, no parking permit. This supports evidence from the Netherlands (e.g. Ligtermoet, 1998; Schreffler, 1996) that GCPs based solely on carsharing but without disincentives achieve only modest changes in modal split, but that the incentive/disincentive combined is (unsurprisingly) a much more potent measure.

6.6 Costs and benefits of GCP measures

For a fuller discussion of empirical research on costs and benefits, the reader is referred to DETR (1999); for a discussion of the conceptualisation and importance of costs and benefits in GCP evaluation, see Rye (1999). Costs and benefits accrue to the organisation, to staff and to society and it is important to disaggregate these.

Only limited cost/benefit data is available from this study: in spite of repeated requests, it was not possible to obtain from HP the costs of their measures. The installation of 2 showers and 20 lockers at the City of Edinburgh Council recently cost £7,000, so this gives some indication of the costs of HP's installations, although it must always be borne in mind that these are very building specific. Michael McBride is the key member of staff working on the HP GCP and he spends approximately 40% of his time on it.

At the RBS, initial staff input to setting up the carshare scheme was significant (see relevant chapter for details) and there was also a £10,000 charge for internal consultancy. Now, the only costs are administration (normally 0.1 FTE administrator) and enforcement, which is carried out by existing staff. Operationally, the scheme imposes additional inflexibility on staff, which is a cost to them but not to the organisation.

Against these costs must be offset the reduced costs of parking provision and maintenance. Studies in the US (e.g. Comsis Corporation, 1994) have often found these to more than outweigh the cash costs of setting up and maintaining a GCP.

Benefits have accrued to HP staff (and other users of Dalmeny station) as a result of the ScotRail discount. Improved cycle facilities are a benefit to cyclists but also to lunchtime joggers who can use them as well. At RBS, existing and new Lothian Buses commuters can enjoy the benefit of reduced season ticket prices and an interest free loan. Finally at HP, 3+ carpools enjoy the best parking spaces.

In conclusion this report shows that the costs of the measures implemented in the case studies are low; considerably lower than building new car parks. However, financial incentive measures and secured bus services can become expensive – the example of the 58 bus from the Gyle illustrates this point very well.

6.7 What is required in groups of companies

This research has studied two examples of groups of companies attempting to work together on GCP issues. Neither is hugely encouraging. At Kirkton Campus, the companies themselves did not get together but were rather convened by the Council. They did not - as a group - share the concern that the Council has about transport in the Campus area. At the Gyle, the companies themselves got together. They continue to meet because they recognise a problem that, whilst it affects them to different degrees, is a common problem nonetheless. However, besides raising awareness of their difficulties, as a group they have achieved relatively little because most have been reluctant to take on additional work that might not be of direct benefit to *their* organisation. Tasks and responsibilities need to be shared out if this is to occur. But perhaps even more vital is someone to carry out those tasks, as Edinburgh Park Management do in NEP, and has been the case in Chester and Stockley Park Business Parks (both good examples of group GCPs). A Transportation Management Association may be the way forward on this front.

6.8 What is required from government

The attitudinal work and the evidence of negotiations with public transport operators indicates that there are many steps that Government could take to both increase the implementation rate of GCPs, and to reduce the problems that GCPs are intended to solve being caused in the first place. These include:

6.8.1 GCP Measures

- A realistic expectation of what the majority of organisations will do in green commuter planning, given that most do not perceive that they suffer operational transport problems.
- Further changing the tax status of GCP measures such that subsidies for public transport use, and vanpools, do not attract income tax.
- A Challenge Fund for measures (see below).

6.8.2 Public transport

- Ensuring that there are resources available from private or public sector to run peak hour only and orbital bus services. This may mean a change in the regulatory framework as such services are unlikely to be operated commercially.
- Informing public transport operators of the market growth that can be achieved through GCPs. This should go beyond the recently-produced DETR guide on this subject.
- Pursuing integrated ticketing.

6.8.3 Land-use planning

The organisations studied for this research are all located out of town in locations that were attractive precisely because of their accessibility by private car and also because the land was cheap and suitable for building modern offices. However, their accessibility is now compromised by their own success. There is therefore a need for government to ensure that at such sites public transport infrastructure is provided before the buildings are in place; and to offer incentives to developers to develop in town and city centres which will remain the most accessible locations by public transport.

6.9 Further work

This project is now as complete as it can be, within the timescale set by the client. However, in terms of overall project objectives, it has been possible to measure the results of a Travel Plan only at one of the case study workplaces, although there is also some anecdotal evidence of mode shift at one other (the Royal Bank). While in this respect, the project has not fulfilled all of its objectives, in relation to the history of travel planning, to achieve even these results within an 18 month timeframe is quite significant – experience in the Netherlands and the US indicates that gathering before and after data on the effect of travel plans is notoriously difficult.

It was not possible to gather more "after" data for two reasons: at Kirkton Campus and at most employers in the Gyle/Edinburgh Park, nothing had happened; and at the Royal Bank, managers were unwilling to ask their staff to complete an "after" survey so soon after the "before" survey because they perceived that the reaction from staff would be too adverse in a situation where few travel benefits had been delivered. However, there may be a case for revisiting at least the Royal Bank, and possibly NEP, at a later stage in order to carry out "after" surveys.

Further research should also be commissioned on the network effects of GCPs; and of the legality and effectiveness of pursuing effective (i.e. target-based) GCPs within the planning system.

In addition, as noted above, it may be worth approaching the organisations in the Gyle/NEP with a view to joint funding of a Transportation Management Association to work full time on their behalf in securing and publicising better public transport and negotiating with operators and the Council.

Finally, for public sector organisations, GCP start up costs can be considerable (e.g. cycle facilities). A GCP "Challenge Fund" for organisations to bid for to fund such items could be a useful and cheap innovation.

REFERENCES

Becker, H.S. (1982) *Culture: A Sociological View* Yale Review Summer 1982 pp 513-27

Çelikel N. and Saleh W., (2000) Evaluation of Employer-based travel demand management measures, UTSG, Liverpool.

COMSIS Corporation (1994) Cost Effectiveness of TDM Programs, prepared for TCRP

DETR (1999) The benefits of Green Transport Plans. A Summary. DETR

Ligtermoet, D, (1998) *Status: Kansrijk* Report to Dutch Ministry of Transport

Luthans, F. (1989) *Organisational Behaviour* 5th Edition, McGraw-Hill International Editions

Mullins, L.J. (1998) *Management and Organisational Behaviour* 5th Edition, Pitman Publishing

Robbins, S.P. (1998) *Organisational Behaviour* 8th Edition, Prentice Hall Inc.

Rye, T. (1997) *TDM in large organisations* Unpublished PhD thesis

Rye, T. (1999) *Evaluating mobility management* Paper to 3rd ECOMM Conference, Muenster

Saleh W (1998) Data envelopment analysis and modelling efficiency

Schein, E.H. (1985) *Organisational Culture and Leadership* San Francisco: Jossey-Bass pp 168-9

Schreffler E. (1996) *The Effectiveness of TDM Measures at Worksites in the US and the Netherlands* Report to Dutch Ministry of Transport, The Hague

Transport Update

20th October 1998

Timetables: Buses & Trains

♦ Public transport timetables continue to be available on the cafeteria notice board and are being maintained as new ones become available.

Rail Travel:

ScotRail - some progress here, in particular with the reductions in season ticket rail fares to Dalmeny but some issues still remain:

♦ **Flexipass** - this proposal has been shelved for the time being as ScotRail believe that this would be very difficult to administer. It is still a preferred option for many rail users.

♦ **Train Scheduling** - more seats / trains are proposed to be in place by the middle of year 2000. Is this soon enough, particularly if we are to see an increase in users through fare reductions?

♦ **Season tickets** - at last we have a reduction: Quote from ScotRail "Having considered the various options that arose from our discussions, a decision has been made to reduce the cost of season tickets on the various Fife flows in order to generate increased usage of the train These reductions are subject to the condition that increases in the numbers travelling are demonstrated over a period of 6 months. On this basis, the offer will be considered for extension". It is therefore imperative that HP employees (and anyone else) are encouraged to use this service and stick with it if we are to continue to take advantage of ScotRail's good will. This fare reduction is for season tickets only and examples of the new weekly rates are given on the next page.

♦ **A free return ticket to Dalmeny** - is still on the cards to promote rail travel and the new fares deal.

Cycling:

♦ City of Edinburgh Development have confirmed that the A90 cycle path upgrade works are scheduled to commence during the first half of 1999.

♦ The shed at B5 is to be extended to increase capacity. General provision for cyclists is being reviewed across the site.

Car sharing:

♦ The scheme has now been operational for a few months and is generally working well. There is still a notice has been placed on the board at the entrance to the cafeteria for carsharers to 'recruit' and publicise their availability and eligibility for the preferred parking proposal. A total of twelve bays (these are the green/white painted reserved bays strategically situated near employee entrances) have now been allocated to those car pools who satisfy the 'three or more people criteria'. These bays are allocated to individuals who have 'registered' with our site security office and drivers have been issued with a numbered green bay pass - anyone who qualifies should contact Irene / Steve on x32256 or Ian McIntosh on x32858.

Transcript Update

Transport Update
20th October 1998

ScotRail – New Weekly Season Ticket Pricing			
Dalmeny: To	Old 7 Day Season	**New 7 Day Season**	Standard Day Return
Edinburgh	18.90	**14.10**	4.70
Waverley	18.90	**14.10**	4.70
South Gyle	11.70	**9.90**	3.30
North	6.20	**6.20**	2.20
Inverkeithin	8.00	**7.80**	2.60
Dalgety Bay	14.40	**10.80**	3.60
Aberdour	18.50	**14.10**	4.70
Burntisland	22.10	**16.50**	5.50
Kinghorn	25.30	**18.90**	6.30
Kirkcaldy	25.30	**18.90**	6.30
Rosyth	8.00	**7.80**	2.60
Dunfermline	17.10	**12.60**	4.20
Cowdenbeat	25.10	**18.30**	6.10
Lochgelly	29.00	**21.30**	7.10
Cardenden	31.30	**24.30**	8.10
Glenrothes	32.90	**24.30**	8.10

APPENDIX 3.2: FURTHER RESULTS FROM HP 1997 STAFF TRAVEL SURVEY

SQF - Employee Transport

The Issues

Our site has experienced significant employee growth over the last few years and this trend will continue for some time. Additionally car ownership per capita is increasing to both a local and national crisis. The car parking facilities on our site are now inadequate and the difficult decision to purchase a plot of land to provide additional spaces has now been taken to address current safety issues. HP cannot continue to support this growth in car parking facilities on site indefinitely. It is imperative that we analyse our employee needs and be ultimately able to ensure that suitable alternative transport is available to service the site. We also have a responsibility to reduce the impact on our environment and this strategy will help curb increases in atmospheric pollution, which together with a reduction in journey fatigue, can ultimately lead to a healthier workforce.

Analysis

Although we could estimate employee travel to work patterns we did not have enough actual data to be able to negotiate with any of the transport providers. A significant proportion of our employees live an acceptable distance to a public transport node, but it is the quality of the service that has driven users to use their own transport. To this end the recent survey was conducted to be able to correlate travel modes, times, problem locations, public transport deficiencies etc. Initial contact with rail transport providers has indicated a certain amount of flexibility and we are optimistic in making some progress here. Other surveys in the UK have identified the obvious but have also highlighted sonic novel ideas. Transport has become such an issue that surveys have generally exceeded a 50% return rate - we were hoping to break HP Bristol's record of 58%!

Objective

Fundamentally, the reduction in the number of employee cars travelling to the site.

How

- Complete the site travelling to work survey
- Publish survey data
- Submit data analysis for negotiations with service providers

The first priority will be the identification of deficiencies in the public transport system, cycling facilities and difficulties in carsharing and develop existing services where possible to match employee

Expectations

- Opened dialogue with the train and bus operators, and the City of Edinburgh Council by the beginning of December 1997. This is not being done in isolation - HP is actively participating in a Chamber of Commerce Transport Forum to represent business interests in tackling local transport issues.
- A 10% reduction in employee car journeys to the site by year2000 (5% by the end of FY98) through the implementation of acceptable public transport strategies.
- An improvement in the facilities offered to cyclists by the end of FY98.

SQF Transport Survey Feedback

Summary

Highlights:
- 68% Survey Return.
- Identified areas for achievable improvements.
- Correlation between information on bus, train, car, cycling, and work start times, routes etc.

Main Points Identified:
- 64% of employees drive on their own to work (over 800 cars on site)
- Usual journey times take less than 30 minutes (although the journey time home is usually 10 minutes longer!).
- Cost, reliability and added journey time are the main deterrents to employees using public transport.
- Factoring the data for the site population, there are just over 100 employees using public transport as their usual mode of transport.
- Cyclists need improved cycle routes and changing / shower facilities.

Opportunities and the Next Steps:
- Target ScotRail for BP Employee discounted tickets and possible alterations to timetable. There are over 300 occasional train users and if we can 'move' half of these to being regular users then this represents 150 fewer car journeys to the site with associated benefits to employees and The Railways.
- Approach the bus services for improvements to their timetable and reliability. There are more
- Potential difficulties to overcome and a 10 - 20% shift to regular use may be more realistic.
- Approach the City of Edinburgh Council with a view to improve selected dangerous routes to the site (the A90 link in particular).
- Offer a Car Share Data base (with preferred parking slot options) for interested employees.

Issues:
- The journey time for most employees is less than 30 minutes door to door - can a public service achieve an acceptable journey time?
- Any direct **financial benefit** offered to employees may have an associated tax liability.

HPSQ Transport Survey Feedback

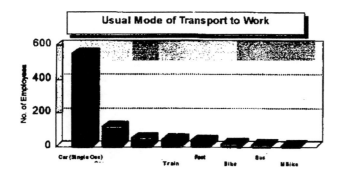

- Few surprises here! There is, however, more car sharing than expected.
- Rail and bus use is disappointingly low.

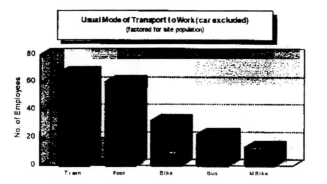

- This data (as a subset of the above) has been factored to reflect the entire employee population (does not include temporary/contract staff) to more clearly reflect on other modes of access to the site.
- A general concern raised is the lack of pedestrian / car segregation, in particular from the north gate to the building entrances.

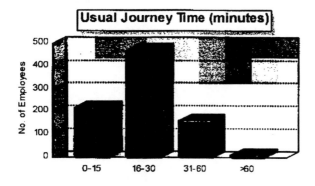

- This is the time taken to travel to work. Indications from most of us who travel on average about 10 miles each way is that it typically takes 10 minutes longer going home.
- This is one of the features offered by a car for someone who doesn't live in a traffic hotspot - is there any other mode of transport that can match this door to door travel time?

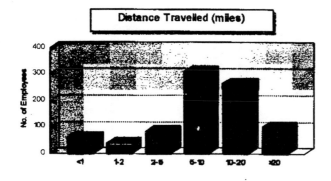

- The location of the site has meant that the average distance travelled by employees is a little over 10 miles each way.
- Comments have included "I chose to live 20 miles away because it used to be so easy to drive to work"!

HPSQ Transport Survey Feedback

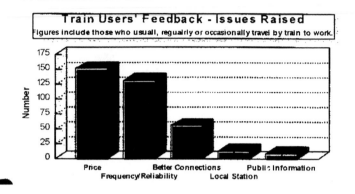

Train Users' Feedback - Issues Raised
Figures include those who usuall, regualrly or occasionally travel by train to work.

- By far the greatest concern and deterrent to rail travel is cost (judging by the additional comments). Feedback suggests that rail travel to work would cost an employee 2 to 3 times as much as a car journey.

- Employees still remember the strikes!

- There are some gaps in the timetables and this will be communicated to Scotrail.

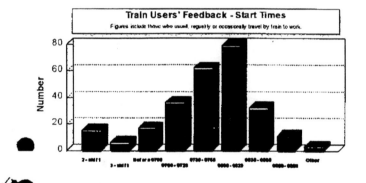

Train Users' Feedback - Start Times
Figures include those who usuall, regualrly or occasionally travel by train to work.

- We can use this data in conjunction with postcode areas to identify and discuss with Scotrail / Railtrack 'areas for opportunity'.

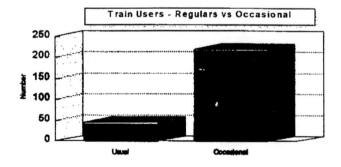

Train Users - Regulars vs Occasional

- If we factor this data for the whole site then we have over 300 occasional rail users. Scotrail have indicated flexibility in price and this is going to be our first strategy.

- What is a realistic objective? Can we target to move 50% of the occasionals to the regular column? If so then a 50% discounted rail fare would still increase Scotrail's respective income by 70%.

HPSQ Transport Survey Feedback

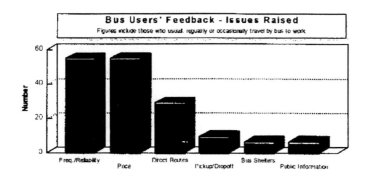

Bus Users' Feedback - Issues Raised
Figures include those who usual, reguarly or occasionally travel by bus to work

- ◆ Although price features as a concern, nearly all additional comments were directed toward the reliability and frequency of the existing service.

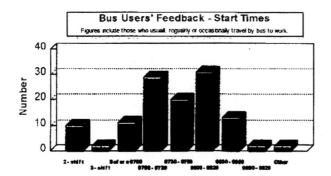

Bus Users' Feedback - Start Times
Figures include those who usual, reguarly or occasionally travel by bus to work.

- ◆ Again, we can use this data in conjunction with postcode areas to identify and discuss areas of opportunity with the new/potential service providers.

- ◆ Employee finish time is more of a challnge as far as the timetable is concerned.

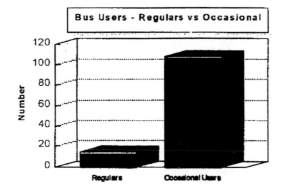

Bus Users - Regulars vs Occasional

- ◆ This is a sad refelction on the quality of the current service. The LRT service has been withdrawn from SQ and all that remains is the regional service now operated under First Bus.

- ◆ Judging survey comments, the first objective will be to ensure that the bus provider can guarantee a service that adhers to the timetable!

- ◆ It may be realistic to assume a movement of only 10% from occasional to regular use.

HPSQ Transport Survey Feedback

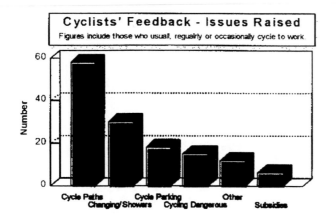

Cyclists' Feedback - Issues Raised

Figures include those who usuall, reguairly or occasionally cycle to work.

- Most comments were directed toward the dangers of cycling via the A90 and over the road bridge. The City of Edinburgh Council has plans for an A90 cycle path 'upgrade' as part of the Millennium Programme.

- Cyclists would also like more site facilities to accommodate changing and bike parking. Motor cyclists used this section to comment on inadequate MBike parking facilities.

- Season/weather influence is nearly as great as distance (lack of daylight in particular).

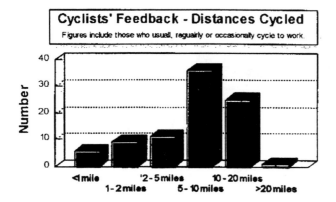

Cyclists' Feedback - Distances Cycled

Figures include those who usuall, reguairly or occasionally cycle to work.

- Season/weather influence is nearly as great as distance (lack of daylight in particular). Distance is the greatest deterrent amongst almost 50% of those who responded.

APPENDIX 3.3: COPY OF PANEL SURVEY FORM AND QUESTIONNAIRE

INTERVIEW QUESTIONS FOR PANEL MEMBERS AT HP

Issues we need to probe:

- Car-sharing - how does it work for them (details of whether they alternate cars, how they pay each other)? What kind of influence has the provision of a parking space been on their choice to carpool(where appropriate)? What are the down and upsides of carpooling? What was their previous mode?
- Reasons for mode choice - why have they ranked them in that particular order? Ask them to expand on issues of particular importance e.g. security?
- Need to probe to assess attitudes to modes they don't currently use and in particular to assess how they think the employer could change any of these aspects through a GCP.
- Cost - what is composed of i.e. how do they regard variable costs? What do they think the cost of public transport actually is if they do not currently use it?
- Attitudes to telecommuting i.e. would they like more of it, what do they think management would think?
- Have they noticed the GCP? How could it be improved/have more influence?

Organisational issues

- Do they see how green commuting fits in with the HP way?
- Do they think their managers really believe in it?
- Are there parallels with any other work-based campaigns e.g. health?

Questions	Interviewer prompts
1. We note that you ranked *x* factor as the most important determinant of your current mode choice. Can you expand on this a little and explain how this mode is the most advantageous for you at the present moment? What are its advantages and, if applicable, disadvantages compared to other modes? 2. Please could you tell us more about what is unacceptable to you about other modes of transport? How would you have to alter your current lifestyle to use a different mode? What impacts would that have? 3. Could HP do anything to encourage you to use a different mode of travel to work [car users]/support you in your current use of public transport, walking or cycling? 4. Should the company take any interest in how its employees get to work and attempt to influence their choice? Or does the responsibility lie completely with the individual employee and with the bodies which provide transport services? 5. You have stated that the costs of your journey to work are £*x* per week. Does this include all the costs of car use/getting to the station/cycle maintenance [etc]? How much would other modes cost? 6. Do you think that car parking at work represents a subsidy to the staff who drive to work which is not given to those who use other modes? 7. Would you like to telecommute some of the time or work a compressed work week? How would your managers react to this? **Organisational issues** 1. Do you think that the way in which people get to work at present causes problems for HP? 2. Do you ever recall your managers or colleagues mentioning green commuting initiatives here at HP? How were they communicated? How often? 3. If you were a manager here would you encourage your employees to consider green commuting? Why/why not? 4. If you were a manager here would you encourage your employees to go to the gym regularly or to strive for a sensible balance between home and work? 5. Do you think your manager cares how you get to work? 6. Do you think HP means what it says about caring for the environment? 7. Does green commuting fit into the HP way? 8. Should HP at SQF charge for parking at work at present and use the money to subsidise the use of other modes? 9. If answer to 8 is no, are there circumstances which you could envisage in the future where it might be justifiable for HP to charge for parking?	*Just remind them about the reasons for the project. Stress that **we are not** attempting to influence their choice of mode*

APPENDIX 3.4 ADDITIONAL COMMENTS FROM PANEL SURVEY

Reason for not using public transport for respondents who car commute and have an option to use public transport by carshare.	
Car share	**Reason for not using public transport**
No	Takes twice as long and combination of bus / walking and train.
No	Distance from home and convenience.
No	Car more flexible-goes when I want: bus/train/walk takes too long
No	Longer journey time, unreliable, overcrowded (train)
No	Mainly cost, it is much more expensive by train and bus, then the times don't suit that well.
No	Convenience of door-to-door transportation - especially in the Edinburgh climate.
No	I would have to first use a bus (3X time of equivalent car journey), then swap over to the train (2X time of equivalent car journey).
No	I have children to drop off at nursery on my way to work and this involves driving to the nursery which is en route to work.
No	Taxi/bus to station then two train journeys (total time approx. 1 to 2 hrs).
No	Local public transport is inconvenient, UNRELIABLE, costly and time consuming. Consists of: walk to nearest bus stop, bus journey, considerable walk to train station, Major disincentive to using public transport is unreliability, both punctuality and mechanical. Both buses and trains are consistently late or are cancelled without warning. Journey has been known to take more than 3 HOURS ! ! !
No	Train times are unsuitable, one at 7:04 then 7:50. If there was one around 7:30 I would consider that.
No	It is ineffective for me to take public transport, due to the travelling time involved. More than 1h30 for a single trip.
No	30 minute walk to nearest railway station and then 2 or 3 trains from Lenzie to Dalmeny stations. Cost ~ £14 per day return.
No	Takes too long, not integrated, not frequent enough.
No	Too expensive. Not reliable enough. Not frequent enough. NOT CONVENIENT.
No	Don't use it because of unpredictable hours, unreliable and uncomfortable public transport.
No	Much longer journey time.
No	The first bus that would take me to work would get me there too late. The nearest train station to me is Cowdenbeath which I would need to drive to but there is no parking available. The next available train stations with parking are either Dunfermline or Dalgety Bay and if I was going to drive that far then I'm as well driving the whole way. When my car is unavailable I can get a lift to Cowdenbeath but that isn't available to me on a regular basis.
No	Long walk from stop to factory, infrequent service.
No	Unreliable (also slow, expensive).
No	Rail season tickets give poor discounts to people with flexible holiday arrangements.
No	Direct bus infrequent. Indirect bus would take at least 1 hour.
No	Have to get a taxi to get the public transport - nearest bus stop is over 1 mile away.
No	Walking distance to public transport, not frequent enough, expensive, not direct to the workplace (buses)
No	Exposed platform, freezing in Winter (Haymarket). Train return times infrequent, still gap between 17.34 & 18.39 I work long hours, and do shopping on way back. Cost of rail travel is excessive. Still cheaper to put petrol in car than pay for train ticket.
No	Flexibility, speed and reliability.
No	Previous bad experiences regarding reliability.
Yes	Too damned expensive.
Yes	Too expensive.
Yes	I live in Musselburgh and work in South Queensferry: Two bus or train journeys are required; one into Edinburgh, and the other to work/home. The time a bus journey would take is prohibitive, approximately 1.75 hours. The cost of using the train is also to ..
Yes	The cost, per day, by public transport is £20 (I commute from Glasgow).
Yes	Cost, time of day that services start, time between service connections, time of journey, weather and overall inflexibility.
Yes	Time and cost.
Yes	Do not use because it would be more expensive and take longer to get to work.
Yes	Strikes, cancellations, late, overcrowding, only once an hour in evening.
Yes	My wife drives by HP on the way to her work and drops me off and she cannot use public transport.

Measures suggested by respondents to include in a Green Commuter Plan, by mode of travel.	
Mode of travel	**Measure(s) for a Green Commuter Plan**
Car (not sharing)	Door-to-door transportation - minibus to Edinburgh stations, or comfortable fast coach service. Pricing that beats the cost of using a car (reflects lower convenience and lower flexibility of public transport). In pricing my journey I only consider the incremental cost of using the car (petrol & extra wear) since the fixed costs are fixed! I need a
Car (not sharing)	Improved rail links outwith main towns.
Car (not sharing)	The creation of a Car Sharing Database, so that individuals can form new carshare groups.
Car (not sharing)	Efforts to maximise co-operation between modes of transport, e.g., all inclusive public transport tickets, direct transport to train stations, PUNCTUALITY, RELIABILITY, clean buses/trains, adequate seating, etc. In short any measure (subsidised if necessary) aimed at improving public transport to the levels already accepted as standard in other European countries, e.g., Germany. UNTIL PUBLIC TRANSPORT OFFERS ACCEPTABLE LEVELS OF COMFORT, CONVENIENCE AND RELIABILITY, IN URBAN/COUNTRY AREAS AS WELL AS IN THE TOWNS, IT WILL CONTINUE TO PROVE DIFFICULT, IF NOT IMPOSSIBLE, TO PERSUADE COMMUTERS TO CHANGE TO USING PUBLIC TRANSPORT.
Car (not sharing)	A better rail service with trains running directly from Falkirk to Dalmeny. Help in setting up a car pool.
Car (not sharing)	I'd like to see the railway line already used for Longannet Power Station to Rosyth, opened up for public transport!
Car (not sharing)	Improved comfort and cleanliness while waiting for and travelling on public transport will always help. Cost must be more competitive than at present. You cannot legislate for unpleasant, abusive and drunk passengers on a public system.
Car (not sharing)	Make provision for commuter trains to carry more cycles. I would like to be in a position to use the train/cycle mix more regularly however cost is also a major factor.
Car (not sharing)	Creation of safe cycleways.
Car (not sharing)	An increase in the Greenways would be beneficial I feel that they work very well. Providing parking at the city limits and then a dedicated bus would also help.
Car (not sharing)	The car costs (with one occupant !!) the same as train and is more convenient. Either the train should get cheaper, or, become more convenient. More flexibility in train season tickets (ie I would prefer to). Design road cycle tracks so that they are safe to use in dark and at commute times. 15 mins between trains - or - a convenient way to determine (from work/home) if the next train is running to time.
Car (not sharing)	More frequent trains and buses.
Car (not sharing)	Make trains work & come & go to schedule.
Car (not sharing)	Company subsidy for public transport travel?
Car (not sharing)	I commute from Kinross - if a train service ran from there I would use it.
Car (not sharing)	Web-based route planner/timetables for buses (like Railway already has)
Car share	While any reduction in train fares is always welcome, they would have to be reduced significantly for me to consider using the train on a regular basis. It would also help if I could get connecting trains without having long waits at Waverley.
Car share	Flat rate fares for journeys that allow changes between buses and trains (cf Toronto). More regular and reliable public transport that starts earlier in the morning and remains frequent until later. Remove company car mileage tax allowances. Integrated
Car share	A REAL reduction in train fares - I do not want to travel to Dalmeny at weekends.
Car share	There should be financial benefit for not using one's car on ones own etc. One should not be libel for more tax as a result of the company subsidising public transport. There is no direct rail service from West Lothian to Dalmeny.
Car share	More showers, facilities for drying cycling clothes.
Car share	Greater incentive for people to carshare.
Cycle/train	Improved and more cycle paths, roads are biggest danger - Newbridge-Dalmeny. When it rains I can't use the paths.
Train	Provision of more trains by ScotRail between 1734 hrs and 1829 hrs
Train	More showering facilities on site for use after cycle to work.
Train/walk	Train timetable still needs to be improved during commuting hours. Need better information at Dalmeny station of train delays etc.
Train/walk	Improve public transport service (frequency, reliability) - stop subsidising car users.
Train/walk	More bus routes: cheaper buses/trains; trains; open up existing around Edinburgh which is currently just used for freight; park & ride facilities in outskirts of Edinburgh.

AGILENT TECHNOLOGIES
STATED PREFERENCE QUESTIONNAIRE

The completion of this survey offers you the opportunity to comment on journey to work issues and to influence the development of an action plan to lead ultimately to a reduction in car use. Benefits include reduced traffic congestion, stress, air pollution levels and may also be financially beneficial to employees. Survey data will be treated in strict confidence. It will be used to decide which measures in the action plan will be most effective and beneficial to employees. It also forms part of a research project for the Scottish Executive which will help to inform their policy on green transport plans and travel to work generally.

SECTION A: ABOUT YOURSELF

Name and department...................

1. Sex   ❐ Male ❐ Female

2. Age   ❐ 18-25   ❐ 26-35   ❐ 36-45   ❐ 46+

3. Job title ....

4. Household income per year
❐ Less than £10 000   ❐ £20 000 - 30 000
❐ £10 000 - 20 000   ❐ £30 000 +

5. Please give your post code minus the last two letters   ....

6. Which of the following do you have access to for your trip to work?
❐ Car
❐ Bike
❐ Bus stop within walking distance. Please tick the box if there is a direct service to workplace ❐
❐ Rail station within walking distance. Please tick the box if there is a direct service to workplace ❐

SECTION B: TRAVEL TO WORK

1. How do you currently travel to work?

Walk		Bus	
Motorbike		Bicycle	
Train		Car on your own	
Taxi		Car pooling – a group takes turns at giving each other lifts to work	
Minibus		Car, as a passenger	
Other			

2. How long does your journey to work normally take, one way, in minutes?

....

What are your usual start and end times?	Shift title	Time	
		Start hh:mm)	End hh:mm)
Not on shift work		:	:
If 2 shift		:	:
		:	:
If 3 shift		:	:
		:	:
		:	:

4. If you travel to work by car, do you have any kind of commitment on the way to/from work which makes you do so?
   ❐ Yes (please specify) ....
   ❐ No

5. If you have changed your mode in the past two years, what was your previous mode ?

Walk		Bus	
Motorbike		Bicycle	
Train		Car on your own	
Taxi		Car pooling – a group takes turns at giving each other lifts to work	
Minibus		Car, as a passenger	
Other			

6. Please specify the reason for changing?

....

....

7. If currently drive or carpool to work, how long do you think it would take you to get to work by public transport and how many times would you have to change, one way?

   Journey time .... Minutes
   Changes.............................
   OR
   ❐ Don't know

SECTION C: SCENARIOS

In this section we are going to offer you some choices about your travel options to work. We would like to know how you would choose between the following options.

1: CARPOOLING

Imagine that there is a computerised carpooling matching service available at your work place. There are enough preferential parking spaces close to office buildings for all car-poolers and there is also a guaranteed/emergency ride home service available for car-poolers, should you have to get home in an emergency, for example to care for a sick child. Please consider each of the following options and decide which you would choose.

Scenario 1: If the preferential parking spaces reserved are offered to "3 or more" car-pooler's cars. *Would you consider to carpool?*

☐ As a car driver
    ☐ Definitely consider
    ☐ Might consider
☐ As a passenger
    ☐ Definitely consider
    ☐ Might consider

☐ No

Scenario 2: If the preferential parking spaces reserved are offered to "2 or more" car-pooler's cars. *Would you consider to carpool?*

☐ As a car driver
    ☐ Definitely consider
    ☐ Might consider
☐ As a passenger
    ☐ Definitely consider
    ☐ Might consider

☐ No

2. CARPOOLING AND PARKING MANAGEMENT

2.1. Reduction on parking spaces

Now assume that number of parking places at work will be reduced for solo drivers, therefore, parking spaces are limited. However, there is a computerised carpooling matching service available. There are enough preferential parking spaces close to the office buildings for all car-poolers and there is also a guaranteed / emergency ride home service available for car-poolers. On the other hand, to be sure of getting a parking place as a solo car driver, you need to arrive to work earlier. Please consider each of the following scenarios and decide which option you would choose.

Scenario 1: You would have to get to work **15 minutes** earlier than your actual starting time. *Would you consider to carpool?*
☐ ☐ As a car driver Y ☐ Definitely consider e ☐ Might consider s ☐ As a passenger ☐ Definitely consider ☐ Might consider
☐ *If so, which mode would you use?* N ☐ car (alone) o ☐ public transport ☐ cycling ☐ walking ☐ other

Scenario 2: You would have to get to work **30 minutes** earlier than your actual starting time. *Would you consider to carpool?*
☐ ☐ As a car driver Y ☐ Definitely consider e ☐ Might consider s ☐ As a passenger ☐ Definitely consider ☐ Might consider
☐ *If so, which mode would you use?* N ☐ car (alone) o ☐ public transport ☐ cycling ☐ walking ☐ other

2.2. Parking charges

Assume that there is a parking charge introduced for solo drivers. However, there is a computerised carpooling matching service available. There are enough preferential parking spaces close to office buildings with guaranteed /emergency ride home service available for car-poolers. As a solo driver you will have to pay a parking fee as shown below. Please consider each of the following scenarios and decide which option you would choose.

Scenario 1: £1 per day per space parking charge. Free parking for car-poolers. *Would you consider to carpool?*

☐ Yes	☐ As a car driver
	    ☐ Definitely consider
	    ☐ Might consider
	 ☐ As a passenger
	    ☐ Definitely consider
	    ☐ Might consider

☐ No	*If so, which mode would you use?* ☐ car (alone) ☐ public transport ☐ cycling ☐ walking ☐ other

Scenario 2: £2 per day per space parking charge. Free parking for car-poolers. *Would you consider to carpool?*

☐ Yes	☐ As a car driver
	    ☐ Definitely consider
	    ☐ Might consider
	 ☐ As a passenger
	    ☐ Definitely consider
	    ☐ Might consider

☐ No	*If so, which mode would you use?* ☐ car (alone) ☐ public transport ☐ cycling ☐ walking ☐ other

Scenario 3: **£3** per day per space parking charge. Free parking for car-poolers. *Would you consider to carpool?*

	☐ As a car driver
	    ☐ Definitely consider
	    ☐ Might consider
	 ☐ As a passenger
	    ☐ Definitely consider
	    ☐ Might consider

	If so, which mode would you use? ☐ car (alone) ☐ public transport ☐ cycling ☐ walking ☐ other

3. CARPOOLING, CHARGING AND TRAVEL ALLOWANCE

Assume that there is a travel allowance which is regular, periodic payments (provided either as a cash payment or as a monthly salary adjustment), to cover employees' commute costs (it does not matter which mode you use) as is done in many German and Dutch companies. There is also a computerised carpooling matching service available. There are enough preferential parking spaces close to office buildings with guaranteed /emergency ride home service available for car-poolers. As a solo car driver you would have to pay your parking fee as shown below. Please consider each of the following scenarios and decide which option you would choose.

Scenario 1: Travel allowance is **£1** per day. Parking fee is a **£1** per space but free for car-poolers. *Would you consider to carpool?*

Yes	☐ As a car driver
	     ☐ Definitely consider
	     ☐ Might consider
	 ☐ As a passenger
	     ☐ Definitely consider
	     ☐ Might consider

No	☐ *If so, which mode would you use?*
	     ☐ car (alone)
	     ☐ public transport
	     ☐ cycling
	     ☐ walking
	     ☐ other

Scenario 2: Travel allowance is **£2** per day. Parking fee is a **£2** per space but free for car-poolers. *Would you consider to carpool?*

Yes	☐ As a car driver
	     ☐ Definitely consider
	     ☐ Might consider
	 ☐ As a passenger
	     ☐ Definitely consider
	     ☐ Might consider

No	☐ *If so, which mode would you use?*
	     ☐ car (alone)
	     ☐ public transport
	     ☐ cycling
	     ☐ walking
	     ☐ other

Scenario 3: Travel allowance is **£3** per day. Parking fee is a **£3** per space but free for car-poolers. *Would you consider to carpool?*

Yes	☐ As a car driver
	     ☐ Definitely consider
	     ☐ Might consider
	 ☐ As a passenger
	     ☐ Definitely consider
	     ☐ Might consider

No	☐ *If so, which mode would you use?*
	     ☐ car (alone)
	     ☐ public transport
	     ☐ cycling
	     ☐ walking
	     ☐ other

2. CARPOOLING, PUBLIC TRANSPORT SUBSIDY AND PARKING CHARGING

Now, assume that your company will subsidise public transport season tickets. On the other hand, there is a parking charge introduced for solo drivers at your work place. There is a carpooling scheme with enough preferential parking spaces close to office buildings with a guaranteed /emergency ride home service available for car-poolers. Please consider each of the following options and decide which one you would choose.

Scenario 1: There is a **£1** parking fee per day but free for car-poolers. Public transport is **50%** cheaper than currently (but the same journey time and frequency). *Would you consider to carpool?*

Yes	As a car driver	
	☐ As a car driver	
		☐ Definitely consider
		☐ Might consider
	☐ As a passenger	
		☐ Definitely consider
		☐ Might consider
No	*If so, which mode would you use?*	
	☐ car (alone)	
	☐ public transport	
	☐ cycling	
	☐ walking	
	☐ other	

Scenario 2: There is a **£2** parking fee per day but free for car-poolers. Public transport is **50%** cheaper than currently (but the same journey time and frequency). *Would you consider to carpool?*

	As a car driver	
	☐ As a car driver	
		☐ Definitely consider
		☐ Might consider
	☐ As a passenger	
		☐ Definitely consider
		☐ Might consider
	If so, which mode would you use?	
	☐ car (alone)	
	☐ public transport	
	☐ cycling	
	☐ walking	
	☐ other	

Scenario 3: There is a **£3** parking fee per day but free for car-poolers. Public transport is **50%** cheaper than currently (but the same journey time and frequency). *Would you consider to carpool?*

☐ Yes	As a car driver	
	☐ As a car driver	
		☐ Definitely consider
		☐ Might consider
	☐ As a passenger	
		☐ Definitely consider
		☐ Might consider
☐ No	*If so, which mode would you use?*	
	☐ car (alone)	
	☐ public transport	
	☐ cycling	
	☐ walking	
	☐ other	

5. PUBLIC TRANSPORT SUBSIDIES

Assume that your company will subsidies public transport season tickets. There is also a carpooling scheme with enough reserved parking spaces close to the office buildings and guaranteed /emergency ride home service is available for car-poolers. Please consider each of the following options and decide which one you would choose.

Scenario 1: There is an interest free loan for purchasing public transport season tickets (but the same journey time and frequency). *Would you consider to use public transport?*	**Scenario 2** : Public transport is 50% cheaper than currently for you (but the same journey time and frequency). *Would you consider to use public transport?*
☐ Yes	☐ Yes
☐ N o	☐ N o
If so, which mode would you use? ☐ car (alone) ☐ car-pooling ☐ cycling ☐ walking ☐ other	*If so, which mode would you use?* ☐ car (alone) ☐ car-pooling ☐ cycling ☐ walking ☐ other

6. VANPOOLING

Assume that a van-pooling scheme will be introduced. Company vans with comfortable seating are given to those who live in the same area (if there are enough people in that area) to travel to work. You will be picked up from home and taken to HP. Each person in the scheme would be responsible for picking up and dropping off the others in a rota system. Please consider each of the following scenarios and decide which option you would choose.

Scenario 1: Cost of use is £1 per day (inclusive). *Would you be using this scheme?*	Scenario 2: Cost of use is £2 per day (inclusive). *Would you be using this scheme?*

Yes   □ Definitely consider
       □ Might consider
	Yes □ Definitely consider
	       □ Might consider

No □ *If so, which mode would you use?* □ car (alone) □ carpooling □ public transport □ cycling □ walking □ other	No □ *If so, which mode would you use?* □ car (alone) □ carpooling □ public transport □ cycling □ walking □ other

7. CYCLING

Assume that improved facilities for cyclists - covered bicycle racks, showers, better changing and drying facilities - are provided in your building. Please consider each of the following options and decide which one you would choose.

Scenario 1: There is a interest free loan for purchasing bike and also company bicycle pool which provides you a bike when/ how long you like. Draws and repair vouchers are available for the cyclists. *Would you consider to cycle to work?*	**Scenario 2**: There is a carpooling scheme available with preferential parking place and a guarantied /emergency ride home service. *Would you consider to cycle to work?*
☐	☐
If yes how many days a week you would cycle?	*If yes how many days a week you would cycle?*
In the summer In the winter	In the summer In the winter
Y ☐ every day ☐ every day	Y ☐ every day ☐ every day
e ☐ once a week ☐ once a week	e ☐ once a week ☐ once a week
s ☐ twice a week ☐ twice a week	s ☐ twice a week ☐ twice a week
☐ ☐ three times a week ☐ three times a	☐ ☐ three times a week ☐ three times a
N week	N week
o ☐ four times a week ☐ four times a	o ☐ four times a week ☐ four times a
week	week
☐ other…………… ☐	☐ other…………… ☐
other……………	other……………
If not always what alternative mode would you use other days?	*If not always what alternative mode would you use other days?*
☐ car (alone)	☐ car (alone)
☐ carpooling	☐ carpooling
☐ public transport	☐ public transport
☐ walking	☐ walking
☐ other	☐ other

Scenario 3: Public transport is 50% cheaper than currently but journey time and the frequency are the same. *Would you be cycling to work?*

☐

If yes how many days a week you would cycle?

In the summer	In the winter
Y	
e ☐ every day	☐ every day
s ☐ once a week	☐ once a week
☐ twice a week	☐ twice a week
☐ three times a week	☐ three times a week
N	
o ☐ four times a week	☐ four times a
☐ other……………	week ☐
other……………	

If not always what alternative mode would you use other days?
☐ car (alone)
☐ carpooling
☐ public transport
☐ walking
☐ other

Scenario 4: There is a £2 parking charge per space per day and public transport 75% cheaper than at the moment. *Would you be cycling to work?*

☐

If yes how many days a week you would cycle?

In the summer	In the winter
Y	
e ☐ every day	☐ every day
s ☐ once a week	☐ once a week
☐ twice a week	☐ twice a week
☐ three times a week	☐ three times a
N	
o ☐ four times a week	☐ four times a
week ☐ other……………	week ☐
other……………	

If not always what alternative mode would you use other days?
☐ car (alone)
☐ carpooling
☐ public transport
☐ walking
☐ other

SECTION D: GREEN TRANSPORT PLAN MEASURES

Please consider the following measures, some of which are already in place while others are planned for or could be implemented. Please consider these measures in terms of their effectiveness (high, medium or low) in reducing your car travel.

	High	Medium	Low
ALTERNATIVES TO CAR			
Computerised carpooling matching on the Intranet			
Increasing number of preferential parking spaces and including new spaces for car-poolers (for 2 or more)			
Formal emergency ride home service for carpoolers			
Company van-pooling scheme			
Company shuttle bus services for those who do not have the direct public transport services to/ from work place			
INCENTIVES			
Financial incentives for those who use alternative modes (public transport, cycling, walking, carpooling etc)			
Interest free loan for purchasing a bicycle			
Travel allowances (cash in hand or tickets or coupons for all employees)			
Special promotions and draws for alternative mode users			
ALTERNATIVE WORK HOURS			
Compressed work hours (10 hours for 4 days, 12 hours for 3 days, etc.)			
Teleworking (working at home for some days)			
PARKING MANAGEMENT			
Parking management (controls, restrictions, reduction or apply parking charging equivalent to travel allowance)			
PROVIDING TRAVEL INFORMATION			
On site transportation co-ordinator (full/ part time co-ordinator who is appointed to give advice to employees on their travel choices and organising events, draws for car-poolers, cyclists, walkers, PT users)			
Online public transport information (time tables, routes, promotions etc.)			
OTHERS (Please specify)			

SECTION E: ALLOCATING THE BUDGET

Now, assume that you are given a budget of 100 units to spend on some alternative packages of Green Transport measures that could be implemented. Please assess these packages in each case, in order of preference and assign some budget to each of them to reflect its effect on how people would travel to work.

EXAMPLE

Budget	Measures
20	Carpooling scheme with computerised matching. Increasing number of preferential parking spaces. Interest free loans for purchasing a bike.
30	Carpooling scheme with computerised matching. Increasing number of preferential parking spaces. Financial incentives for public transport users
50	Carpooling scheme with computerised matching. Increasing number of preferential parking spaces. Emergency / guarantied home ride service

Case 1:

Budget	Measures
	Carpooling scheme with computerised matching. Increasing number of preferential parking spaces. Interest free loans for purchasing a bike.
	Carpooling scheme with computerised matching. Increasing number of preferential parking spaces. Financial incentives for public transport users
	Carpooling scheme with computerised matching. Increasing number of preferential parking spaces. Emergency / guarantied home ride service

Case 2:

Budget	Measures
	Improve cycling facilities (racks, showers, drying and changing facilities) Interest free loan for purchasing a bicycle Negotiation with the public transport service providers to get better service to/from work place Special promotions and draws for cyclists
	Company shuttle bus services for those who do not have the direct public transport services to/ from work place Subsidising public transport season tickets, loans for season tickets Special promotions and draws for all public transport users
	Special promotions and draws for car-poolers Carpooling scheme with computerised matching. Increasing number of preferential parking spaces. Emergency / guarantied home ride service

Case 3:

Budget	Measures
	Travel allowances (cash in hand or tickets or coupons for all employees) Parking management (controls, restrictions, reduction or apply parking charging equivalent to travel allowance) Increasing number of preferential parking spaces.
	Travel allowances (cash in hand or tickets or coupons for all employees) Parking management (controls, restrictions, reduction or apply parking charging equivalent to travel allowance) Interest free loans for purchasing a bike.
	Carpooling scheme with computerised matching. Travel allowances (cash in hand or tickets or coupons for all employees) Parking management (controls, restrictions, reduction or apply parking charging equivalent to travel allowance)

Thank you very much for your time. The information you have given will be used to help to develop HP's Green Transport Plan and will also inform the Scottish Executive's policy on green transport plans. A copy of the full project report will be sent to Michael McBride at HP at the end of March but if you would like your own copy please email t.rye@napier.ac.uk after that time.

APPENDIX 3.6 TECHNICAL APPENDIX ON HP 1999 TRAVEL SURVEY

Hewlett Packard, South Queensferry
Travel to Work Surveys 1997 and 1999

1. The surveys – an overview

In 1997, of approximately 1,200 travel to work questionnaires were sent to staff, 856 were returned, coded and analysed by HP. This survey was designed exclusively by Hewlett Packard (HP). Napier University received a copy of the data and this has been used to allow comparisons to be made with the more recent survey undertaken in 1999.

In 1999 to meet HP's own requirements and to assist in this study, the survey was repeated. The survey form was designed as a joint venture between HP and Napier University. Just over 1,300 forms were sent out and 683 returns were received. To meet the requirements of both partners, the 1999 survey requested more information from staff than was the case in the 1997 survey.

Copies of the survey forms used are to be found …..

2: Usual mode of travel

Table 2.1 summarises the responses and it is clear that there has been a significant change in travel patterns with a 6% reduction ($p<0.05$) in car-based travel together with an 8% rise ($p<0.05$) in rail travel. Indeed the proportion of staff travelling by rail has more than doubled from 5% in 1997 to 13% in 1999.

Table 2.1: Usual mode of travel to work - summary

number of responses/percentage

Usual mode of travel to work	1997		1999		%age change	Chi-square*	5% sig?
	Number	%age	Number	%age			
Car-based	721	84.4%	535	78.3%	-6.1%	9.034	yes
Train	45	5.3%	89	13.0%	7.8%	29.709	yes
Other (known)	88	10.3%	59	8.6%	-1.7%	1.033	no
Total (known modes)	854	100.0%	683	100.0%	-	-	-

* Chi-square test is with Yates' correction

Although there has been some small observed movements in other modes (see Table 2.1), none is significant ($p<0.05$). In terms of car-based travel it is significant ($p<0.05$) that the largest reduction – representing 80% of the total reduction – is related to staff members who used to travel on their own in a car.

1

Table 2.2: Usual mode of travel to work - details

number of responses/percentage

Usual mode of travel to work	1997		1999		%age change	Chi-square*	5% sig?
	Number	%age	Number	%age			
Car, on your own.	550	64.4%	405	59.3%	-5.1%	3.982	yes
Train.	45	5.3%	89	13.0%	7.8%	29.707	yes
Car, with others (car sharing).	118	13.8%	81	11.9%	-2.0%	1.122	no
Car, passenger.	53	6.2%	49	7.2%	1.0%	0.741	no
Foot.	41	4.8%	27	4.0%	-0.8%	0.460	no
Bicycle.	21	2.5%	15	2.2%	-0.3%	0.028	no
Motorbike.	8	0.9%	12	1.8%	0.8%	2.679	no
Bus.	13	1.5%	5	0.7%	-0.8%	1.421	no
Other.	5	0.6%	0	0.0%	-0.6%	2.408	no
Unknown.	2	-	0	-	-	-	-
Total (known modes)	854	100.0%	683	100.0%	-	-	-

* Chi-square test is with Yates' correction

3. Distance of journey to work

Respondents were asked to state the distance of their journey to work and the results are shown in Table 3.1

This question was posed in different terms between the two surveys and for this reason statistical tests have not been carried out because they may not be robust. However, descriptively, there does appear to be little difference in terms of distance travelled to work between the two surveys.

Table 3.1: Distance of journey to work for all modes

number of responses/percentage

Distance band	1997		1999	
	Number	%age	Number	%age
Up to 1 mile	60	7.0%	34	5.0%
1 - 2 miles	38	4.4%	23	3.4%
2 - 5 miles	81	9.5%	54	7.9%
5 - 10 miles	309	36.1%	277	40.6%
10 - 20 miles	267	31.2%	202	29.6%
Over 20 miles	101	11.8%	78	11.4%
Missing value			15	
Total	856	100.0%	683	97.8%

The majority of staff (57%) travel less than 10 miles to work the largest proportion of which travel between 5 an 10 miles.

Tables 3.2(a) and 3.2(b) cross-tabulate distance by usual mode of travel and by cumulative percentage for the 1999 data.

Table 3.2: Usual mode by distance (1999)

number

Usual mode	No response	Number in Distance Group (miles)						
		<1	1-2	2-5	5-10	10-20	>20	Total
Bicycle.			1	2	11	1		15
Bus.		1		1	1	2		5
Car, on your own.	3	6	12	35	159	138	52	402
Car, passenger.			2	2	30	12	3	49
Car, with others (car sharing).		3	1	4	29	24	20	81
Foot.		24	3					27
Motorbike.					6	5	1	12
Train.	12		4	10	41	20	2	77
Total	15	34	23	54	277	202	78	668

percentage

Usual mode		Cumulative %age by distance (miles)					
		<1	1-2	2-5	5-10	10-20	>20
Bicycle.	-	0%	7%	20%	93%	100%	100%
Bus.	-	20%	20%	40%	60%	100%	100%
Car, on your own.	-	1%	4%	13%	53%	87%	100%
Car, passenger.	-	0%	4%	8%	69%	94%	100%
Car, with others (car sharing).	-	4%	5%	10%	46%	75%	100%
Foot.	-	89%	100%	100%	100%	100%	100%
Motorbike.	-	0%	0%	0%	50%	92%	100%
Train.	-	0%	5%	18%	71%	97%	100%
Total		5%	3%	8%	41%	30%	12%

With the exception of people who walk and travel by bus, the statistical mode (ie the most commonly reported Distance Group) is between 5-10 miles.

The cumulative percentages show that people who car share travel longer distances and this reflects comments received during the interview survey which suggested that for longer distance travel, car-sharing combines the benefits of lower costs (fuel and vehicle maintenance) with less stress because driving is shared.

Table 3.3 cross-tabulates distance by occasional modes of travel and by cumulative percentage for the 1999 data.

Table 3.3: Occasional mode by distance (1999)

Occasional mode	No response	Number in Distance Group (miles)						
		<1	1-2	2-5	5-10	10-20	>20	Total
Bicycle.	1	4	4	8	29	14	1	60
Bus.	2	2	3	8	35	19	5	72
Car, on your own.	2	11	6	5	50	19	18	109
Car, passenger.	3	1	1	6	50	25	9	92
Car, with others (car sharing).		2		4	22	18	4	50
Foot.		8	9	2	4			23
Minibus.					1	1		2
Motorbike.				3	2	3	1	9
No alternative transport used.	6	7	6	14	79	73	37	216
None stated.			1		1	1		3
Other					1			1
Taxi.			1	1	2			4
Train.	1			11	86	60	20	177
Total	15	35	31	62	362	233	95	818

Occasional mode		Cumulative %age by distance (miles)					
		<=1	<=2	<=5	<=10	<=20	>20
Bicycle.		7%	13%	27%	75%	98%	100%
Bus.		3%	7%	18%	67%	93%	100%
Car, on your own.		10%	16%	20%	66%	83%	100%
Car, passenger.		1%	2%	9%	63%	90%	100%
Car, with others (car sharing).		4%	4%	12%	56%	92%	100%
Foot.		35%	74%	83%	100%	100%	100%
Minibus.		0%	0%	0%	50%	100%	100%
Motorbike.		0%	0%	33%	56%	89%	100%
No alternative transport used.		3%	6%	13%	49%	83%	100%
None stated.		0%	33%	33%	67%	100%	100%
Other		0%	0%	0%	100%	100%	100%
Taxi.		0%	25%	50%	100%	100%	100%
Train.		0%	0%	6%	55%	89%	100%
Total		4%	8%	16%	60%	88%	100%

The distances for occasional modes show broadly similar trends. Staff, however, who live further afield are more likely not to use an alternative mode transport.

4. Time taken to travel to work

Respondents were asked to state how long it took them to get to work. The results are shown in Table 4.1

This question was posed in different terms between the two surveys and for this reason statistical tests have not been carried because they may not be robust. However, descriptively, there does appear to be little difference in terms of time taken to travel to work between the two surveys.

Table 4.1: Time to travel to work

number of responses/percentage

Time band	1997		1999	
	Number	%age	Number	%age
0-15 minutes	217	25.4%	166	24.3%
16-30 minutes	467	54.6%	385	56.4%
31-60 minutes	160	18.7%	118	17.3%
Over 60 minutes	12	1.4%	14	2.0%
Total	856	100.0%	683	100.0%

Both surveys show that the majority of staff continues to take less than half an hour to travel to work. Fewer than one in five take over thirty minutes.

5. Occasional mode when usual mode is unavailable

Respondents were asked to state their occasional (alternative) mode(s) of transport to work if their usual mode was not available. Some significant differences between the surveys were observed (Table 5.1 refers).

Table 5.1: Occasional modes* used to travel to work

number of responses/percentage

Occasional Mode	1997		1999		%age change	Chi-square**	5% sig?
	Number	%age	Number	%age			
Train	219	20.7%	178	21.4%	0.7%	0.168	no
No alternative transport used	212	20.0%	222	26.7%	6.6%	11.902	yes
Car, passenger	164	15.5%	95	11.4%	-4.1%	6.274	yes
Car, on your own	130	12.3%	111	13.3%	1.0%	0.550	no
Bus	108	10.2%	74	8.9%	-1.3%	0.794	no
Car, with others (car sharing)	81	7.7%	50	6.0%	-1.7%	1.728	no
Bicycle	77	7.3%	61	7.3%	0.0%	0.016	no
Foot	49	4.6%	23	2.8%	-1.9%	3.955	yes
Other	9	0.9%	10	1.2%	0.3%	0.979	no
Motorbike	9	0.9%	9	1.1%	0.2%	0.552	no
Total	1058	100.0%	833	100.0%	-		

* Respondents were asked to tick no more than two occasional modes

** Chi-square test is with Yates' correction

Significantly (p<0.05) smaller proportions of staff responded that they walked or travelled as a car passenger. A significantly (p<0.05) larger proportion indicated that they adopted no alternative mode of transport.

Table 5.2 sets out a cross-tabulation of occasional mode by usual mode and it shows that patterns do change by usual mode. Obviously, occasional modes are a matter of practicality for people and alternative choices of travel may not always include the possibility of using all other modes.

Table 5.2: Occasional mode by usual mode (1999) - Summary

number of responses/percentage

Usual Mode	Occasional mode	Number	%age
Non-car user.	Car User.	97	54.2%
	Non-car user.	47	26.3%
	No alternative transport used.	34	19.0%
	None stated.	1	0.6%
	Total	**179**	**100.0%**
Car User.	Non-car user.	304	46.8%
	No alternative transport used.	187	28.8%
	Car User.	157	24.2%
	None stated.	1	0.2%
	Total	**649**	**100.0%**

It is clear that the majority (54%) of non-car users use some form of car-based travel to get to work as an occasional mode.

The responses indicate that almost half (47%) of the car users use a non-car mode of occasional travel. However, between a quarter and a third (29%) state that they use no alternative mode of travel. This aspect was not the subject of any supplementary questions and just how this was achieved is not known. The remaining quarter (24%) share or get a lift to work.

Table 5.3 shows these data in more detail. For all non-car modes, the most common occasional mode is as a car user. As car users , the largest proportion of people (53%) will remain with car travel of some sort; however, on in four report that they would travel by train. By the same token a majority of train users will use a car as an occasional mode.

Table 5.3: Occasional mode by usual mode (1999) - Details

Usual Mode	Occasional mode	Number	%age
Bicycle.	Car, all users.	13	56.5%
	Train.	8	34.8%
	Bus.	1	4.3%
	Bus.	1	4.3%
	Total	**23**	**100.0%**
Bus.	Car, all users.	3	60.0%
	Foot.	1	20.0%
	No alternative transport used.	1	20.0%
	Total	**5**	**100.0%**
Car, all users.	No alternative transport used.	187	28.8%
	Train.	166	25.4%
	Car, all users.	157	24.2%
	Bus.	56	8.6%
	Bicycle.	53	8.2%
	Foot.	18	2.8%
	Motorbike.	8	1.2%
	Taxi.	3	0.5%
	None stated.	2	0.3%
	Other.	1	0.2%
	Total	**650**	**100.0%**
Foot.	Car, all users.	16	51.6%
	No alternative transport used.	8	25.8%
	Bicycle.	2	6.5%
	Foot.	2	6.5%
	Bus.	2	6.5%
	None stated.	1	3.2%
	Total	**31**	**100.0%**
Motorbike.	Car, all users.	7	41.2%
	Bus.	5	29.4%
	Train.	4	23.5%
	Bicycle.	1	5.9%
	Total	**17**	**100.0%**
Train.	Car, all users.	58	56.3%
	No alternative transport used.	25	24.3%
	Bus.	12	11.7%
	Bicycle.	5	4.9%
	Taxi.	1	1.0%
	Foot.	1	1.0%
	Motorbike.	1	1.0%
	Total	**103**	**100.0%**
Total	**Total**	**829**	-

7

6. Encouragement to use public transport

The survey forms included a question requesting information about changes that would encourage staff to use public transport. These are shown in Table 6.1.

More detailed information was requested in this respect in the 1999 survey and this may have encouraged wider ranging responses from staff.

Significantly (p<0.05), a smaller proportion responded that discounted tickets available at work were seen as an encouragement. This finding may be because ScotRail cut the cost of rail season tickets to Dalmeny by up to 25% between the times of the two surveys. The degree of additional encouragement, therefore, afforded by further reductions in rail travel costs may have diminished.

Table 6.1: Changes* that would most encourage public transport use (1997 & 1999)

number of responses/percentage

Occasional Mode	1997 Number	1997 %age	1999 Number	1999 %age	%age change	Chi-square**	5% sig?
More direct bus routes.	189	14.2%	154	13.8%	-0.5%	0.080	no
More frequent/reliable bus service.	182	13.7%	131	11.7%	-2.0%	2.018	no
Better bus shelters (lighting etc).	13	1.0%	13	1.2%	0.2%	0.404	no
Discounted tickets/passes available at work.	294	22.2%	200	17.9%	-4.3%	6.644	yes
More convenient pick-up/drop-off points.	75	5.7%	56	5.0%	-0.6%	0.382	no
More frequent/reliable train service.	219	16.5%	215	19.2%	2.7%	3.244	no
Better connections between the station and home or work.	147	11.1%	112	10.0%	-1.1%	0.624	no
Public transport information.	24	1.8%	10	0.9%	-0.9%	3.070	no
Nothing would encourage me to travel to work by public transport.	151	11.4%	102	9.1%	-2.3%	3.115	no
Other.	33	2.5%	126	11.3%	8.8%	78.330	yes
of which:							
I don't require to use public transport.			50				
cleaner buses and trains.			28				
cheaper public transport			11				
other (<10 responses)			19				
No response			18				
Total	1327	100.0%	1119	100.0%			

* Respondents were asked to tick no more than two changes

** Chi-square test is with Yates' correction

There was a significant increase (P<0.05) in the proportion of staff who responded that an 'other' change would encourage use of public transport. This result may be related to the way in which the question was formulated in which a greater emphasis was placed on other factors in 1999 survey.

Table 6.2 shows these data stratified by car and non-car user. Here, almost the whole range of responses show significant differences (P<0.05).

Table 6.2 Changes* that would most encourage public transport use by car and non-car user (1999)

number of responses/percentage

Encouragement to Use Public Transport	Car User		Non-Car User		%age change	Chi-square**	5% sig?
	Number	%age	Number	%age			
More direct bus routes	144	16.5%	10	4.1%	-12.4%	23.524	yes
Discounted tickets/passes available at work	141	16.1%	59	24.2%	8.1%	9.015	yes
More frequent/reliable train service	126	14.4%	89	36.5%	22.1%	61.332	yes
More frequent/reliable bus service	118	13.5%	13	5.3%	-8.2%	11.508	yes
Better connections between station and home/work.	102	11.7%	10	4.1%	-7.6%	11.278	yes
Nothing would encourage me to travel to work by public transport.	99	11.3%	3	1.2%	-10.1%	22.221	yes
More convenient pick-up/drop-off points	51	5.8%	5	2.0%	-3.8%	4.965	yes
I don't require to use public transport	28	3.2%	22	9.0%	5.8%	16.515	yes
Cleaner buses and trains	18	2.1%	10	4.1%	2.0%	4.148	yes
Better bus shelters (lighting etc)	10	1.1%	3	1.2%	0.1%	0.202	no
Public transport information	4	0.5%	6	2.5%	2.0%	11.041	yes
Better bus interchange facilities	7	0.8%	2	0.8%	0.0%	0.190	no
Other	15	1.7%	6	2.5%	0.7%	1.060	no
None stated	12	1.4%	6	2.5%	1.1%	2.196	no
Total	875	100.0%	244	100.0%			

* Respondents were asked to tick no more than two changes

** Chi-square test is with Yates' correction

The differences here show just how sensitive opinion is to the current mode of transport. Non-car users see discounted tickets, service information and train reliability as greater encouragements than do car users. Bus service improvements, however, are seen as a greater encouragement by car users. This latter observation may reflect the fact that only a few non-car users travel by bus and don't see bus service improvements as making any real difference to their travel choice. Whereas car users may simply regard such improvements as another travel option.

7: Main reasons for driving to work

Respondents were asked to state their main reason(s) for driving to work. The results tabulated in Tables 7.1 and 7.2 refer only to responses received from those who drive to work on their own.

Table 7.1 shows the responses by reason and indicates only one significant change. A significantly ($p<0.05$) smaller proportion saw the fact that they had a company car to be a reason to drive to work. This finding is in line with the decreasing number of company cars at HP resulting from financial incentives to give up company cars. This, of course, does not mean that in giving up a company car staff travel by a non-car mode.

Table 7.1: Summary of main reason(s)* for driving to work on one's own

number of responses/percentage

Reason for driving a car to work	1997 Number	1997 %age	1999 Number	1999 %age	Chi-square**	5% sig?
Car essential to perform job.	23	3.7%	14	2.3%	1.576	no
Company car.	37	5.9%	9	1.5%	15.745	yes
Dropping/collecting children.	60	9.6%	55	9.0%	0.060	no
Lack of acceptable alternative etc	387	61.9%	403	66.2%	2.612	no
Other.	118	18.9%	128	21.0%	1.022	no
Total	625	100.0%	609	100.0%	-	-

* Respondents were asked to tick no more than two reasons

** Chi-square test is with Yates' correction

Table 7.2 shows these data in detail.

Table 7.2: Main reason(s)* for driving to work on one's own in detail

number of responses/percentage

Reason for driving a car to work	1997 Number	1997 %age	1999 Number	1999 %age	1999 grouped Number	1999 grouped %age
Car essential to perform job.	23	3.7%	14	2.3%	14	2.3%
Company car.	37	5.9%	9	1.5%	9	1.5%
Dropping/collecting children.	60	9.6%	55	9.0%	55	9.0%
Lack of acceptable alternative.	387	61.9%	215	35.3%		
No direct service available			155	25.5%	403	66.2%
Don't like public transport.			33	5.4%		
Other.	118	18.9%	-	-	-	-
habit			34	5.6%		
flexibility			24	3.9%		
social/family commitments			13	2.1%	128	21.0%
bus/train takes longer than car			18	3.0%		
cheaper than public transport			10	1.6%		
other (<10 responses)			29	4.8%		
Total	625	100.0%	609	100.0%	609	100.0%

* Respondents were asked to tick no more than two reasons

** Chi-square test is with Yates' correction

8: Willingness to car-share?

Staff were asked if they would be willing to car-share. The results are set out in Tables 8.1 and 8.2

Interestingly, there appears to be a real shift in attitudes to car-sharing. If the "not knowns" are excluded from the responses, a significantly (p<0.05) smaller proportion of staff would now wish to car-share; this is matched by a significantly (p<0.05) larger proportion who would now not wish to car-share. This result may reflect that some "saturation" level has now been reached in car-sharing potential.

Table 8.1: Willingness to car-share: all respondents

number of responses/percentage

Willing to car share	1997		1999		%age change	Chi-square*	5% sig?
	Number	%age	Number	Number			
No	383	44.7%	372	54.5%	9.7%	8.615	yes
Yes	365	42.6%	259	37.9%	-4.7%	7.990	yes
No response	108	12.6%	52	7.6%	-	-	-
Total	856	100.0%	683	100.0%	-	-	-

* Chi-square test is with Yates' correction and calculated on of known responses only

Table 8.2 shows that over 60% of staff who drive to work in a car on their own are unwilling to car-share. This result is significant (p<0.05).

Table 8.2: Willingness to car-share: respondents travelling by car on their own

number of responses/percentage

Willing to car share	1997		1999		%age change	Chi-square*	5% sig?
	Number	%age	Number	Number			
No	294	53.5%	248	61.8%	8.4%	6.295	yes
Yes	244	44.4%	148	36.9%	-7.5%	13.686	yes
No response	12	2.2%	5	1.2%	-	-	-
Total	560	100.0%	401	100.0%	-	-	-

* Chi-square test is with Yates' correction and calculated on of known responses only

9: Encouragement to car-share

Respondents were asked to identify what might encourage them to car-share.

Table 9.1(a) refers only to those staff members who expressed a willingness to share. Descriptively, there does appear to be little difference in what would encourage car-sharing between the two surveys. Statistically (p<0.05), there is also no difference between the two surveys.

Table 9.1(b) refers only to the 1999 survey and compares responses stratified by those willing and not willing to car-share. There are significant (<0.05) differences between the two groups with those unwilling to share seeing emergency ride home as a greater encouragement than do those willing to share. Help in finding a partner is seen as being more important by those willing to share.

Table 9.1: Encouragement* to car-share

(a) Comparison of respondents willing to car-share (1997-1999).

number of responses/percentage

Encouragement to car share	1997		1999		%age change	Chi-square**	5% sig?
	Number	%age	Number	%age			
Help in finding car share partners with similar work patterns.	255	54.0%	176	54.2%	0.1%	0.012	no
Emergency ride home service if let down by car driver.	156	33.1%	108	33.2%	0.2%	0.017	no
Reserved parking for car sharers.	47	10.0%	31	9.5%	-0.4%	0.006	no
Others (all <10 responses each)	14	3.0%	10	3.1%	0.1%	0.091	no
Total	472	100.0%	325	100.0%	-	-	-

(b) Comparison of respondents willing and not willing to car-share (1999 only)

number of responses/percentage

Encouragement to car share	Willing		Not willing		%age change	Chi-square**	5% sig?
	Number	%age	Number	%age			
Help in finding car share partners with similar work patterns.	176	54.2%	61	37.7%	-16.5%	11.130	yes
Emergency ride home service if let down by car driver.	108	33.2%	70	43.2%	10.0%	5.083	yes
Reserved parking for car sharers.	31	9.5%	15	9.3%	-0.3%	0.004	no
Others (all <10 responses each)	10	3.1%	16	9.9%	6.8%	11.282	yes
Total	325	100.0%	162	100.0%	-	-	-

* Respondents were asked to tick no more than two encouragements

** Chi-square test is with Yates' correction

10: Encouragement to cycle

Respondents were asked to identify what would most encourage them to cycle to work. The results are shown in Tables 10.1 and 10.2.

There does appear to be a change in the responses (see Table 10.1). A significantly (p<0.05) smaller proportion indicated that improved cycle parking would assist. On the other hand, a significantly (p<0.05) higher proportion indicated other factors that would encourage them to cycle.

The smaller proportion now seeing improved cycle parking as an encouragement may be the result of the installation of new bicycle sheds around the site between the dates of the two surveys: cycle parking may now be less of an issue to staff.

Table 10.1: Encouragement* to cycle to work - all responses

number of responses/percentage

Encouragement to cycle	1997 Number	1997 %age	1999 Number	1999 %age	%age change	Chi-square**	5% sig?
Improved cycle paths on the journey to work.	224	23.8%	214	27.2%	3.3%	2.687	no
Improved cycle parking at workplace.	41	4.4%	18	2.3%	-2.1%	4.998	yes
Improved changing/locker facilities at workplace.	108	11.5%	84	10.7%	-0.8%	0.221	no
Arrangements for subsidised bicycle purchase/supply	50	5.3%	41	5.2%	-0.1%	0.000	no
Nothing would encourage me to cycle to work	484	51.5%	375	47.6%	-3.9%	2.455	no
Other.	33	3.5%	56	7.1%	3.6%	12.094	yes
Of which:							
living closer to work			24	3.0%			
better weather			19	2.4%			
other (< 10 responses each)			13	1.6%			
Total	940	100.0%	788	100.0%			

* Respondents were asked to tick no more than two encouragements

** Chi-square test is with Yates' correction

Table 10.2 splits the information by car and non-car users for 1999. Here, there are some significant (p<0.05) differences with more car users stating nothing would encourage them to cycle. Smaller proportions of car users see improved cycle paths and improved changing/locker facilities as encouragements to cycle

Table 10.2: Encouragement* to cycle by car and non-car user (1999)

number of responses/percentage

Encouragement to Cycle	Car User Number	Car User %age	Non-Car User Number	Non-Car User %age	%age change	Chi-square**	5% sig?
Nothing would encourage me to cycle to work.	318	52.1%	57	32.0%	-20.1%	23.860	yes
Improved cycle paths on journey to work.	150	24.6%	64	36.0%	11.4%	9.908	yes
Improved changing/locker facilities at workplace.	58	9.5%	26	14.6%	5.1%	4.315	yes
Arrangements for subsidised bicycle purchase/supply.	30	4.9%	11	6.2%	1.3%	0.711	no
Other: living closer to work	22	3.6%	2	1.1%			
Other: better weather	13	2.1%	6	3.4%			
Improved cycle parking at work.	9	1.5%	9	5.1%			
Other: safe road conditions	7	1.1%	2	1.1%			
Other: Time allowance	2	0.3%	0	0.0%			
Other: better facilities on trains, cheaper fares for cyclists	1	0.2%	1	0.6%			
Total	610	100.0%	178	100.0%			

* Respondents were asked to tick no more than two encouragements

** Chi-square test is with Yates' correction

11: Change of travel mode on a regular basis

This question was not asked in the 1997 survey. Tables 11.1 and 11.2 display the responses.

Interestingly, some 21% indicated that they do change mode on a regular basis.

Table 11.1: Change of travel mode on a regular basis - 1999 only

	number of responses/percentage	
Change travel mode	Number	%age
No	528	77.3%
Yes	142	20.8%
No response	13	1.9%
Total	683	100.0%

Free-text reasons were also requested for any change and these indicate that such changes can relate to:

- a small number of trips (over a year or season) being undertaken by a different mode because of regular after-work activities or extreme weather conditions

- trips taken by a different mode because of regular specific family or work commitments

- a completely different pattern of travel (over many months) relating to weather conditions (eg walking or cycling during summer months)

- trips undertaken by a different mode (eg bicycle) on a regular basis to maintain fitness

These findings are summarised in Table 11.2.

Table 11.2 Summary of modes adopted by reason for respondents indicating that they regularly change mode.

Number

Regular alternative modes	Reason	Number
bicycle/foot	seasonal/weather	2
bus/foot	seasonal/weather	2
bus/motorcycle	seasonal/weather	1
car/bicycle	seasonal/weather	36
car/bicycle	personal	8
car/bicycle	none stated	2
car/bus	personal	5
car/bus	work	1
car/car	personal	6
car/car	work	4
car/car	seasonal/weather	1
car/foot	seasonal/weather	5
car/foot	personal	1
car/foot	none stated	1
car/motorcycle	seasonal/weather	8
car/train	seasonal/weather	7
car/train	personal	5
car/train	work	5
car/train	none stated	6
motorcycle/cycle	none stated	1
motorcycle/foot	none stated	1
train/bicycle	seasonal/weather	5
train/bicycle	personal	2
train/bus	convenience	3
train/motorcycle	seasonal/weather	2
train/motorcycle	none stated	2
unknown	n/a	20
Total	All	142

12. Change of mode since 1ˢᵗ January 1998

Staff were asked to indicate if they had changed mode since 1ˢᵗ January 1998 and if so, a number of additional questions to determine previous mode, whether or not the change resulted from an HP initiative and the reason for the change. This question was asked only in the 1999 survey.

One in seven (14%) respondents indicated that they had changed mode since January 1998 (Table 12.1 refers).

**Table 12.1: Change of mode since
1st January 1998**

number of responses/percentage

Change of mode	Number	%age
No	588	86.1%
Yes	94	13.8%
No response	1	0.1%
Total	683	100.0%

Only a small proportion (2.3%) stated that they had done so because of a specific initiative by Hewlett Packard (Table 12.2 refers).

**Table 12.2: Was change because of a specific
initiative promoted by HP?**

number of responses/percentage

HP initiative?	Number	%age
Not applicable	588	86.1%
No	77	11.3%
Yes	16	2.3%
No response	2	0.3%
Total	683	100.0%

Table 12.3 shows a cross-tabulation of current and previous modes. Although there were some possible illogical responses (eg respondents indicating that they had changed mode from train to train), by far the largest area of change (22 No) was from *car, on your own* to *train*.

Those changes stated by staff to be because of an HP initiative are shown in Table 12.4. Half of those (8 No) related to the change from *car, on your own* to *train*. Although, in total, 22 people made the same change, 14 did not record that it was because of an HP initiative. Reasons for this are not known.

Table 12.3: Current and previous modes if mode changed since 1st January 1998

number

Current mode	Previous mode	Number
Bicycle	Bus	1
	Car, on your own	4
	Car, with others (car sharing).	1
	Train	2
Bus	Car, on your own	1
Car, on your own	Bicycle	1
	Bus	5
	Car, on your own	8
	Car, passenger.	4
	Car, with others (car sharing).	5
	Foot	2
	Train	7
Car, passenger.	Car, on your own	2
	Car, passenger.	1
	Train	1
Car, with others (car sharing).	Car, on your own	8
	Car, with others (car sharing).	3
	Train	1
Foot	Car, on your own	5
Motorbike.	Car, on your own	1
	Train	1
Train	Bus	3
	Car, on your own	22
	Car, with others (car sharing).	2
	Foot	1
	Train	1
Total	All modes	93

Table 12.4: Current and previous modes if mode changed since 1st January 1998 and if promoted by an HP initiative

number

Current mode	Previous mode	Number
Car, on your own	Bus	1
	Car, on your own	1
	Car, with others (car sharing).	1
Car, passenger.	Car, passenger.	1
Car, with others (car sharing).	Car, with others (car sharing).	2
Train	Bus	1
	Car, on your own	8
	Train	1
Total	All modes	16

Staff were asked to record as many reasons as applied for the change of mode and these are cross-tabulated with car and non-car users in Table 12.5.

Of the 14% who changed mode, the responses given relate to a number of different reasons. To summarise, 193 reasons were given and the most common reasons given were to reduce the cost of travel (19%) and to reduce the stress of travel (18%). Being "greener" and to reduce the time of travel were other noted responses (11% each).

Table 12.5: Reason(s)* for change of mode by previous and current modes

number/percentage

Reason for change of mode	Previous Mode:	Car user		Non-car User			
	Current Mode:	Non-car	Car	Non-car	Car	Total	%age
To reduce cost of travel.		15	11	5	5	36	18.7%
To reduce stress of travel.		19	8	5	3	35	18.1%
To be "greener".		12	6	2	1	21	10.9%
To reduce time of travel.		8	3	4	6	21	10.9%
Because of change of address.		8	4	2	5	19	9.8%
To improve health.		8	6	3	2	19	9.8%
Because of change in family circumstances.		6	7		4	17	8.8%
To improve reliability of travel.		4	4	1	4	13	6.7%
Other: change in shift.		1	3		1	5	2.6%
Other: bad service quality.		3		1		4	2.1%
Other: bought a car.					2	2	1.0%
Other: more fun.			1			1	0.5%
Total		84	53	23	33	193	100.0%

* Respondents were asked to tick as many as applied.

The largest response was 19 people who reported that they switched form car to non-car modes to reduce stress.

To improve health was stated by 10% of respondents. A similar proportion indicated that they had moved house. Changes in family circumstances and to improve reliability of travel were also mentioned.

13: Measures implemented by HP to encourage change of travel mode

Respondents were asked to identify - and give an effectiveness score to - measures implemented to encourage people to change or keep to the way they travel to work. The analysis has been carried out for all responses and also stratified by current mode of travel (see Table 13.1). A score of 3 was assigned to high effectiveness, 2 to medium and 1 to low effectiveness. Average scores have been calculated.

Table 13.1: Perceived effectiveness and scores for initiatives implemented by HP

(a) Current mode: all modes
number

Measure implemented	Effectiveness			None stated	Total	Score*
	High	Med	Low			
Discounted train tickets	94	146	70	28	338	2.06
Improved cycle parking.	26	120	158	36	340	1.57
Preferential parking spaces for car sharers	36	159	214	49	457	1.56
Car sharing scheme.	19	166	210	44	438	1.52
Improved changing/locker facilities at workplace.	13	67	112	15	207	1.48
None stated				124	124	
Other.				1	1	
Other: Flexible work hours	1				1	
Total	188	657	764	297	1906	1.64

(b) Current mode: car on own
number

Measure implemented	Effectiveness			None stated	Total	Score*
	High	Med	Low			
Discounted train tickets	43	86	53	19	200	1.94
Improved cycle parking.	17	81	101	25	224	1.58
Preferential parking spaces for car sharers	20	106	139	36	300	1.55
Car sharing scheme.	14	103	136	28	281	1.52
Improved changing/locker facilities at workplace.	8	41	81	12	142	1.44
None stated				70	70	
Total	102	416	510	189	1217	1.60

(c) Current mode: train
number

Measure implemented	Effectiveness			None stated	Total	Score*
	High	Med	Low			
Discounted train tickets	38	26	4	2	70	2.50
Car sharing scheme.	0	15	20	5	40	1.43
Preferential parking spaces for car sharers	3	19	13	4	39	1.71
Improved cycle parking.	2	13	15	3	33	1.57
Improved changing/locker facilities at workplace.	0	10	5	1	16	1.67
None stated				9	9	
Other.				1	1	
Total	43	83	57	25	208	1.92

(d) Current mode: cycle
number

Measure implemented	Effectiveness			None stated	Total	Score*
	High	Med	Low			
Discounted train tickets	1	6	1	1	9	2.00
Improved cycle parking.	0	4	4	1	9	1.50
Improved changing/locker facilities at workplace.	0	2	3	1	6	1.40
Car sharing scheme.	0	2	5	1	8	1.29
Preferential parking spaces for car sharers	0	1	6	1	8	1.14
None stated				3	3	
Total	1	15	19	8	43	1.49

(e) Current mode: car-share or car passenger
number

Measure implemented	Effectiveness			None stated	Total	Score*
	High	Med	Low			
Discounted train tickets	11	19	8	3	41	2.08
Improved cycle parking.	6	18	27	6	57	1.59
Preferential parking spaces for car sharers	9	28	42	8	87	1.58
Improved changing/locker facilities at workplace.	4	8	17	1	30	1.56
Car sharing scheme.	3	36	39	8	86	1.54
None stated				26	26	
Other: Flexible work hours	1				1	
Total	34	109	133	52	328	1.64

* Score is average value for response where High=3, Medium=2 and Low=1 (None stated is excluded).

For all response taken together the average score for all measures is 1.64 with discounted train tickets having the highest value at 2.08. Other average scores are all close to 1.5.

A similar pattern is evident for respondents who travel on their own in a car. Here, the average score for all measures is 1.60 with discounted train tickets having the highest value at 1.94. Other average scores are all close to 1.5.

A rather different pattern emerges for train users. The average score for all measures is 1.92 with discounted train tickets having the highest value at 2.50. Preferential parking for car-sharers and improved changing/locker facilities are scored more highly than users of other modes at 1.71 and 1.67 respectively.

Cyclists scored discounted rail tickets most highly at 2.00 but did not see improved cycle parking (1.50) or improved changing/locker facilities (1.40) as being particularly effective.

Respondents who car-share or travel as a car passenger again scored discounted rail tickets most highly at 2.08. Other average scores are close to 1.5. Preferential parking spaces for car-sharers are not seen to particularly effective with a score of 1.56.

14. Willingness to distribute home postcode

Respondents were asked if they would be willing for their home postcode to be used for the purpose of distributing information about staff members seeking car-sharing opportunities and for bus/rail development and discounts. The results are cross-tabulated by willingness to distribute postcode and Council area in Table 14.1.

Overall 62% of staff responding were willing to have their postcodes distributed. There was some variation in the responses by Council area but no clear pattern is evident.

Table 14.1: Willingness to distribute home postcode for car-sharing and public transport discounts by Council area (1999)

number of responses/percentage

| Council | Use of Postcode for distribution? | | | | %age | |
	Yes	No	No response	Total	of Total	"Yes"
Edinburgh	177	94	16	287	42.0%	61.7%
Fife	110	47	4	161	23.6%	68.3%
West Lothian	58	38	1	97	14.2%	59.8%
Falkirk	24	32	2	58	8.5%	41.4%
Midlothian	8	6		14	2.0%	57.1%
Glasgow	9	3		12	1.8%	75.0%
South Lanarkshire	7	1		8	1.2%	87.5%
Perth and Kinross	6	2		8	1.2%	75.0%
Stirling	6	1		7	1.0%	85.7%
Unknown Council Area		5		5	0.7%	0.0%
North Lanarkshire	5	1		6	0.9%	83.3%
Clackmannanshire	4	1		5	0.7%	80.0%
East Lothian	3	2		5	0.7%	60.0%
East Dunbartonshire	2	1		3	0.4%	66.7%
East Renfrewshire	2	1		3	0.4%	66.7%
Scottish Borders	1	1		2	0.3%	50.0%
Dundee	2			2	0.3%	100.0%
Total	424	236	23	683	100.0%	62.1%

Table 14.2 shows similar information for postcode sectors where the number of responses is 10 or more. Again some differences are evident but no clear pattern emerges.

Table 14.2: Willingness to distribute home postcode for car-sharing and public transport discounts by Postcode Sector* (1999)

number of responses/percentage

| Postcode Title | Postcode Sector | Use of Postcode for distribution? | | | | %age |
		Yes	No	No response	Total	"Yes"
South Queensferry/Dalmeny	EH309	18	28	10	56	32.1%
Bo'ness	EH519	9	21	1	31	29.0%
Fife Area	KY119	21	7		28	75.0%
Linlithgow Bridge	EH497	13	12		25	52.0%
Inverkeithing	KY111	12	6	2	20	60.0%
Dunfermline	KY127	11	4		15	73.3%
East Craigs/Clerwood	EH128	10	4		14	71.4%
Linlithgow	EH496	6	6		12	50.0%
Bo'ness	EH510	7	6	1	14	50.0%
Shandon	EH111	9	3		12	75.0%
Saline	KY129	7	4		11	63.6%
Meadows/Tollcross	EH3_9	7	1	2	10	70.0%
Inverleith	EH3_5	10	1	1	12	83.3%
Blackhall	EH4_3	7	3		10	70.0%

APPENDIX 3.7 1997 AND 1999 HP TRAVEL SURVEY FORMS

Travelling to Work: An Employee Survey

Car ownership is increasing and the nation is facing a traffic crisis. Economic measures are expected to be introduced, such as the taxation of car parking, in an attempt to reduce car journeys to work. Our site has experienced significant employee growth over the last few years and this trend will continue for some time. The car parking facilities on our site are now inadequate and the difficult decision to purchase a plot of land to provide additional spaces has now been taken to address current safety issues

The completion of this survey offers you the opportunity to comment on the site's work journey issues and to influence the development of an action plan to ultimately lead to a reduction in car use. Perceived benefits include reduced traffic congestion, stress, and air pollution levels and may also be financially beneficial to employees. Survey data will be treated in confidence and we encourage you to return completed forms to Rosemary Scott, HR Department, by Monday 6th October 1997.

4. How long does it normally take you to get to work?

- ○ 0 - 15 minutes
- ○ 16 - 30 minutes
- ○ 31 - 60 minutes
- ○ Over 60 minutes

1. What is your Work Pattern / Usual Start Time?

- ○ 2 - Shift
- ○ 3 - Shift
- ○ Before 07:00
- ○ 07:00 - 07:29
- ○ 07:30 - 07:59
- ○ 08:00 - 08:29
- ○ 08:30 - 08:59
- ○ 09:00 - 09:30
- ○ Other (please specify)

....

- ○ Not normally based at South Queensferry

5. Which of the following do you occasionally use instead of your usual form of transport? (PLEASE TICK NO MORE THAN 2)

- ○ Bus
- ○ Bicycle
- ○ Car, on your own
- ○ Car, with others (car sharing)
- ○ Car, passenger
- ○ Foot
- ○ Motorbike
- ○ Train
- ○ Other (please specify)

....

- ○ No alternative transport used

2. How do you usually travel to work? (PLEASE TICK ONE ONLY)

- ○ Bus
- ○ Bicycle
- ○ Car, on your own
- ○ Car, with others (car sharing)
- ○ Car, passenger
- ○ Foot
- ○ Motorbike
- ○ Train
- ○ Other (please specify)

....

6. Which of the following changes would most encourage you to use public transport? (If you already travel to work by public transport, which would you most like to see?) (PLEASE TICK NO MORE THAN 2)

- ○ More direct bus routes
- ○ More frequent/reliable bus service
- ○ Better bus shelters (lighting etc)
- ○ Discounted tickets / passes available at work
- ○ More convenient pickup/dropoff points
- ○ More frequent/reliable train service
- ○ Better connections between the station and home or work
- ○ Public transport information
- ○ Other (please specify)

....

- ○ Nothing would encourage me to travel to work by public transport (please comment)

....
....

3. How far do you travel to work?

- ○ Up to 1 mile
- ○ Over 1 mile and up to 2 miles
- ○ Over 2 miles and up to 5 miles
- ○ Over 5 miles and up to 10 miles
- ○ Over 10 miles and up to 20 miles
- ○ Over 20 miles

7. If you drive a car to work, what is your main reason for doing so? (PLEASE TICK NO MORE THAN 2)

- O Car essential to perform job
- O Company car
- O Dropping / collecting children
- O Lack of an acceptable alternative
- O Other (please specify)

....

8. Would you be prepared to car share?

- O Yes
- O No (please comment)

....
....
....
....

9. Which of the following would most encourage you to car share? (PLEASE TICK NO MORE THAN 2)

- O Help in finding car share partners with similar work patterns
- O Emergency ride home service if let down by car driver
- O Reserved parking for car sharers
- O Other (please specify)

....
....
....

10. Which of the following changes would encourage you cycle to work? (PLEASE TICK NO MORE THAN 2)

- O Improved cycle paths on the journey to work
- O Improved cycle parking at workplace
- O Improved changing/locker facilities at workplace
- O Arrangements for subsidised bicycle purchase/supply
- O Other (please specify)

....

- Nothing would encourage me to cycle to work (please comment)

....

11. In the interest of reducing atmospheric pollution wou you consider the use of:

- O Electric vehicles?
- O Alternative fuel powered vehicles (such as Compressed Natural Gas Vehicles)?
- O Other?(please comment)

....
....

12. Do you have any additional comments about your tr to work patterns or local transport issues?

....
....
....
....
....
....
....
....
....
....
....
....
....
....
....

13. Home Postcode (for geographical interpretations)

....

Thank you for taking time to complete this survey. Results will be published in the next issue of Quip and posted on the site notice boards. Please contact Rosemary Scott (Ext. 33068) if you should have any additional comments to assist us in the development appropriate action plan for the site.

Travelling to Work:
An Employee Survey

This is a follow-up survey to the one undertaken in 1997 on travelling to work. Many of you will be aware of how useful it was in making some real improvements.

Car ownership is increasing and transport is becoming a major issue nationally. Measures may be introduced, such as the taxation of car parking, in an attempt to reduce the number of car trips to work. Our site has experienced significant employee growth over recent years and this trend will continue for some time. This may present problems here at South Queensferry.

The completion of this survey offers you the opportunity to comment on journey to work issues and to influence the development of an action plan to lead ultimately to a reduction in car use. Benefits include reduced traffic congestion, stress, air pollution levels and they may also be financially beneficial to employees. Survey data will be treated in strict confidence and we encourage you to return your completed form to Michael McBride, SQF94SF, EHS Department by 30th November 1999, although late replies will be gratefully accepted.

1 What are your usual start and end times?	Shift title	Time	
		Start (hh:mm)	End (hh:mm)
Not on shift work		:	:
If 2 shift		:	:
		:	:
If 3 shift		:	:
		:	:
		:	:

2 How do you usually travel to work? (Please tick one only)	✔
Bus	
Bicycle	
Car, on your own	
Car, with others (car sharing)	
Car, passenger	
Taxi	
Foot	
Motorbike	
Train	
Minibus	
Other	

3 How far do you travel to work?		.	miles

4 How long does it usually take to get to work?		minutes

5 Which of the following do you occasionally use to get to work instead of your usual form of transport? (Please tick no more than two)	✔
Bus	
Bicycle	
Car, on your own	
Car, with others (car sharing)	
Car, passenger	
Taxi	
Foot	
Motorbike	
Train	
Minibus	
Other	
No alternative transport used	

6 Which of the following changes would most encourage you to use public transport? (If you already travel to work by public transport, which would you most like to see?) (Please tick no more than two)	✔
More direct bus routes.	
More frequent/reliable bus service.	
Better bus interchange facilities.	
Better bus shelters (lighting etc).	
Discounted tickets/passes available at work.	
More convenient pick-up/drop-off points.	
More frequent/reliable train service.	
Better connections between station and home/work.	
Public transport information.	
Cleaner buses and trains.	
Others: please state	
I don't require to use public transport.	
Nothing would encourage me to travel to work by public transport.	

7 If you drive a car to work, what is your main reason for doing so? (Please tick no more than two)	✔
Car essential to perform job.	
Company car.	
Dropping/collecting children.	
Lack of acceptable alternative.	
No direct service available.	
Habit	
Don't like public transport.	
Other: please state	

8 Would you be prepared to car share? (Please tick one only and give your reason(s) if you responded "No")	✔
Yes.	
No. Please state your reason(s) in box below.	

9 Which of the following would most encourage you to car share? (Please tick no more than two)	✔
Help in finding car share partners with similar work patterns.	
Emergency ride home service if let down by car driver.	
Reserved parking for car sharers.	
Other: please state	

Travelling to Work:
An Employee Survey

10	Which of the following would most encourage you to cycle to work? (Please tick no more than two)	✔
Improved cycle paths on the journey to work.		
Improved cycle parking at workplace.		
Improved changing/locker facilities at workplace.		
Arrangements for subsidised bicycle purchase/supply		
Other: please state		
Nothing would encourage me to cycle to work		

11	Home Postcode (if you are unable or don't wish to provide your full postcode, filling at least the shaded areas would be helpful)

eg

E	H	5	8		7	F	X

12	Would you be happy for your postcode to be used for the purpose of distributing information about staff members seeking car sharing opportunities and for bus/rail route development and discounts?	✔
Yes		
No		

13	Do you change your travel mode on a regular basis either in keeping with changes in personal circumstances or because of the season/weather?	✔
Yes		
No		
If "Yes" please give details		

Please go to Question 14 top right

14	Have you changed your usual mode of transport to work since 1 January 1998?	✔
Yes (go to Q15)		
No (go to Q18)		

15	Did you change your usual mode because of a specific initiative promoted by HP?	✔
Yes		
No		

16	How did you usually travel to work before you changed mode? (Please tick one only)	✔
Bus		
Bicycle		
Car, on your own		
Car, with others (car sharing)		
Car, passenger		
Taxi		
Foot		
Motorbike		
Train		
Minibus		
Other		

17	Why did you change mode? (Please tick as many as apply and give any other reason(s) for the change)	✔
To reduce cost of travel		
To reduce time of travel		
To reduce stress of travel		
To improve reliability of travel		
To improve health		
To be "greener"		
Because of change of address		
Because of change in family circumstances (eg child care)		
Other: please state		

18	Which of the following measures have HP/Agilent managers and staff implemented to encourage people to change or to keep to the way they travel to work? (Please tick all that apply)	✔	If ticked, how effective do you think the measure has been for HP and staff?		
			High	Medium	Low
Car sharing scheme					
Improved cycle parking					
Improved changing/locker facilities at workplace.					
Preferential parking spaces for car sharers					
Discounted train tickets					
Other: please state					
What else could HP do to encourage you or colleagues to use other modes of transport to work?					

Have you answered Questions 14-17?

Thank you for your time

APPENDIX 4.1: REPORT ON KIRKTON CAMPUS FROM BICS, PANEL SURVEY QUESTIONNAIRE AND PUBLIC TRANSPORT GUIDE 1999

(Includes questionnaire survey sent out to employers)

KIRKTON CAMPUS

PROPOSED GREEN COMMUTER FORUM

Synopsis:

Project : Setting up of Green Commuter Forum, Kirkton Campus, Livingston, West Lothian.

This report essentially sets out the methods used to interest senior representatives of Companies based on Kirkton Campus, Livingston in the concept of 'Green Commuting' and to 'encourage' them to attend the Inaugural Meeting of the Kirkton Campus Green Commuter Forum. Details of the Questionnaire used and the level of response obtained are given and the outcome of the Inaugural Meeting is reported.

B.I.C.S.

Planning, Highways & Traffic Consultancy

2/3 Fettes Rise,
Edinburgh EH4 1QH

Tel: 0131 552 7O57
Mobile: 07775 780155

**Project : Setting up of Green Commuter Forum, Kirkton Campus,
Livingston, West Lothian.**

Reference : We were initially invited to submit proposals for consultancy work associated with the setting up of a Green Commuter Forum on Kirkton Campus by West Lothian Council, Strategic Planning and Transportation (WLC) in August 1998. At the same time West Lothian Council had approached the Scottish Executive to assist with funding of the project. We submitted our proposal with indicative costs to West Lothian Council in a letter dated 1 September 1998. After a meeting at the Scottish Executive attended by representatives from the Scottish Executive Central Research Unit (SO) and West Lothian Council the Scottish Executive, in a letter dated 2 November 1998, offered us a contract for the work, substantially on the basis of our proposal. This was duly accepted.

Review: WLC provided a list of Companies based on Kirkton Campus and the number of employees in each Company. This indicated that there were 66 No. Companies of which 22 No. employed more than 50 people on site.
In accordance with our contract, our initial efforts were directed to:-

1 . Contacting Senior Staff in Companies employing more than 50 staff (22No.) by telephone requesting a meeting to explain the Proposal (for a Green Commuter Forum on Kirkton Campus).

4. Contacting the remaining Companies (44No.) by letter, enclosing a letter of introduction from WLC, briefly explaining the Proposal
5. Preparation and approval of a Questionnaire to be sent/handed to all Companies listed, which would allow assessment of their attitude to green Commuting generally and to the Proposal in particular.

It had been agreed with WLC that the boundaries of Kirkton Campus would be the River Almond in the north, Alderstone Road in the east, Charlesfield Road in the south and Charlesfield Strip in the west. On this basis it soon became apparent that 18 No. Companies on the initial list were not in fact located on Kirkton Campus although only one of these 18 employed more than 50 staff.

Response to Questionnaire

A letter enclosing a copy of the Questionnaire was sent to each Company employing less than 50 staff on 15 November 1998.

Meetings with Senior Staff in Companies employing more than 50 staff commenced on 16 November 1998 and a copy of the Questionnaire was left with each Company with a request for its completion and return. 25 Firms returned completed Questionnaires only 3 of which were completely negative. 12 (of 19) were returned by Companies employing more than 50 staff and 13 (of 27) by Companies employing less than 50 staff.

A copy of the Questionnaire and a summary of the returns are attached.

At an early stage, it became evident that, whilst the larger firms were, by and large, enthusiastic for and supportive of the setting up of a Green Commuter Forum, they were less than enthusiastic about a meeting of the Forum in December because of the level of activity required before the Christmas holidays. We advised SO of this in our letter of 1 December 1998 and it was agreed that the target date for the Inaugural Meeting of the Forum should be mid-January 1999.

By 21 December 1998 we had completed the series of visits and met with Senior Managers of 18 of the 21 Companies with more than 50 employees. In every case enthusiasm was expressed and support pledged for the setting up of a Forum. Of the remaining 3 Firms, one indicated that they had no interest, one returned the Questionnaire sent to their subsidiary, expressing support and the third expressed a degree of support without commitment.

In agreement with SO and WLC, the date of the Inaugural Meeting of the Forum had been set for 21 January 1999 at 4.00 p.m. in the Conference Suite, Almondvale Stadium, Livingston.

At a meeting in the Scottish Executive on 12 January 1999, it was agreed that, in addition to the 49 No. Companies based on Kirkton Campus, formal invitations should be sent to the Chief Executive of West Lothian Chamber of Commerce, the Manager of Kirkton Estates and Cadence Ltd. These were dispatched on 13 January 1999. The meeting also agreed the agenda for the Inaugural Meeting and that Councillor Tony Kinder, Chairman of the Strategic Services Committee of West Lothian Council should be invited to address the Forum.

In the period between fixing the date of the Forum and despatch of the Formal Invitations, we contacted several of the representatives of the Companies we had visited to give advance notice of the date of the Forum and also to invite them to consider whether they would be prepared to serve or be represented on any Steering Group or Executive Committee set up by the Forum.

The Forum

A copy of our report on the Inaugural Meeting of the Forum is attached. The Meeting was attended by 16 No. representatives of Companies based on Kirkton Campus in addition to Councillor Tony Kinder, representatives of SO, WLC and Napier University.

After the formal presentations and a period of discussion, it was established that there was a general wish for a joint initiative to solve problems and improve conditions on Kirkton Campus. However, there was a distinct lack of volunteers willing to chair or serve on the Executive Committee. It was suggested from the floor that the only way forward was to appoint an 'Honest Broker' to drive the project forward. The meeting was also informed that, in a similar situation in Edinburgh the Chamber of Commerce had provided a 'Facilitator'. It was therefore agreed that West Lothian Chamber of Commerce should be invited to accept the position.

After approval by SO and WLC, the Note of the Inaugural Meeting was circulated to the 50 No. Companies invited to attend the Forum in addition to West Lothian Chamber of Commerce and Kirkton Estates.

On 15 February 1999, we contacted the Chief Executive of the Chamber of Commerce and arranged to meet him to explain the proposals and provide as much background information as possible, to enable him to consider our invitation. At that meeting, he indicated his complete sympathy with the objectives of the Forum and that, subject to certain guarantees in respect of support from WLC, he was not averse to acceding to our request. A further meeting has been arranged with WLC representatives to clarify the position.

Recommendations:

6. Consideration should be given to the possible benefits of extending the remit of Kirkton Campus Forum to include Companies in Livingston Village and Kirkton North.

7. Where a business, such as Kirkton Campus Estates, stands to benefit substantially from the success of a Forum, they should be 'encouraged' to take a pro-active role in its setting up and attempting to ensure its success.

8. Assuming the successful establishment of a Forum for Kirkton Campus, that consideration should be given to the establishment of Forums in other similar areas of Livingston.

B.Ireland
Consultant
File. MS Word – KCForum

KIRKTON CAMPUS

PROPOSED GREEN COMMUTER FORUM

QUESTIONNAIRE

Company _____

	YES	NO
Do you operate a shift system?		
Do you operate 'Flexitime'?		
Do you consider you have adequate employee parking at present?		
Do you have space for additional parking if required?		
Do you plan to create additional parking in the near future?		
Do you plan to create additional parking in the long term?		
Would you be interested in encouraging your staff to consider alternative forms of transport?		
Would you be interested in actively encouraging alternative forms of transport by :-		
a) Providing facilities for cyclists?		
b) Designating parking spaces for carsharers?		
c) Subsidising transport to/from your site?		
Would you support the establishment of a Green Commuter Forum for Kirkton Campus?		
Do you have any data on modes of transport used by staff to reach your site?		
Would you be prepared to assist in the collection of travel data?		
Would you be prepared to co-operate in monitoring change in transport usage?		

Signature

Name

Designation

Please return completed form to :- B.I.C.S., 213 Fettes Rise Edinburgh EH4 1 QH

KIRKTON CAMPUS GREEN COMMUTER FORUM – Questionnaire

Company	Shift System Operated	Flexitime operated	Existing Parking Adequate	Space for Additional Parking	Plans for Additional Parking in Near Future	Plans for Additional Parking in Longer Term	Encourage Staff to Consider Alternative Transport	Actively Encourage Alternative Transport	Support Green Commuter Forum	Travel Data Available at Present	Prepared to Collect Travel Data	Prepared to Monitor Change
Award	Y	N	Y	N	N	N	Y	?	?	N	Y	Y
Banta	Y	N	N	Y	Y	?	Y	?	Y	N	Y	Y
Bioscot	N	N	Y	Y	Y	Y	Y	?	Y	N	Y	Y
Burr-Brown	N	Y	Y	Y	N	Y	Y	?	Y	N	Y	Y
City Info	N	Y	Y	Y	N	N	Y	Y	Y	N	N	Y
Compac	N	N	Y	Y	N	N	N	N	?	N	N	N
Diag. Insts.	N	Y	Y	N	N	N	N	N	Y	N	N	N
Diag. Sonar	N	N	Y	Y	N	N	N	N	N	N	N	N
Edin. Sensors	N	N	Y	N	?	Y	Y	N	Y	Y	Y	Y
Ethicon	Y	Y	Y	Y	N	N	Y	Y	Y	N	Y	Y
Flexco Pack.	?	N	N	N	N	Y	Y	?	Y	Y	Y	Y
Grundfos	N	N	Y	Y	N	N	N	N	N	N	N	N
Intelligent App.	N	Y	N	N	N	N	Y	N	Y	Y	N	N
Konika	N	N	Y	Y	N	N	Y	Y	?	N	N	Y
Logic Office	N	N	Y	Y	N	N	Y	N	Y	N	N	N
Magnum	N	N	Y	Y	N	N	Y	Y	Y	Y	Y	Y
Neopost	N	N	Y	Y	N	N	N	N	N	Y	N	N
Quintiles	N	N	Y	Y	N	Y	Y	Y	Y	N	Y	Y
Rood Tech.	Y	N	Y	Y	N	N	Y	Y	Y	Y	N	Y
RoyalBank	Y	N	Y	N	N	N	Y	?	Y	N	Y	Y
Scot. Coal	N	Y	Y	Y	N	N	Y	?	Y	Y	Y	Y
Seiko	N	N	Y	N	N	N	?	N	?	N	?	?
Silva	Y	N	Y	N	N	Y	Y	Y	Y	Y	Y	Y
Sky TV	Y	Y	N	Y	N	N	Y	Y	Y	N	Y	Y
Wisdom	N	Y	Y	N	Y	Y	Y	Y	Y	Y	Y	Y

APPENDIX 4.2 – KIRKTON CAMPUS 2000 TRAVEL GUIDE

Why do we need Travel Plans?

The basic answer is that things never remain the same especially in Livingston. You may consider traffic conditions around Kirkton Campus are not too bad at the moment. One thing is certain, they are not going to improve and will probably get considerably worse. HFA Traffic consultants have been carrying out assessment work for West Lothian Council trying to predict the traffic consequences of all the proposed development in the Kirkton area. The results indicate that many of the junctions in Kirkton Campus and all the junctions on Alderstone Road will become congested, with long queues forming at peak times.

This is not surprising as the workforce in Kirkton Campus is set to double in the next five years.

The Council for its part will be looking at the junctions and will be trying to increase their capacity and reduce queues. The extent and rate this is done will depend on available finance. But this is only part of the answer. You can help yourself by thinking about how you travel to work and how you can avoid using the car by yourself to travel to and from work.

Companies moving into the area are being asked, as part of their planning approval, to instigate Green Commuter Plans. These plans encourage companies to look at ways of reducing the number of cars being driven to their premises and to set targets to reduce the numbers of workers driving by themselves to work.

Who to contact for help

For bus and train information contact:

West Lothian Travel Helpline,
County Buildings,
Linlithgow
(01506) 775288

For advice on general transportation issues and Green Commuting issues contact:

Alastair Short
Team Leader Transportation
West Lothian Council
(01506) 775292

For advice on working with other companies on Kirkton Campus contact:

John Bennett
Chief Executive
West Lothian Chamber of Commerce
(01506) 777937

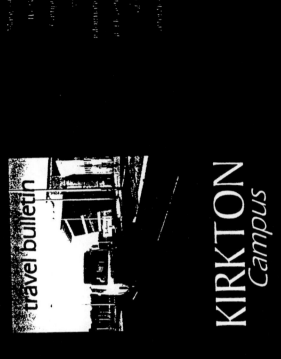

travel bulletin

KIRKTON
Campus

West Lothian Council

West Lothian Chamber of Commerce

February 2000

What is being done?

There is no point in carrying out surveys if nothing is going to be achieved. The Chamber of Commerce is very keen to see practical measures being instigated. Some of the measures are already in place or about to be implemented are:

- Free bus service to Kirkton Campus from Livingston North and Livingston South for rail users.

- An express bus service to and from Edinburgh serving Kirkton Campus directly is being proposed (West Lothian Council is preparing a bid to The Scottish Executive)

- West Lothian bus timetables distributed to various companies.

- Leaflet giving all bus services to Kirkton Campus now available.

- A shuttle bus service to Livingston centre at lunch time has just been launched, and is doing a good trade.

Play your part!

There is a limit to what the Chamber of Commerce and the Council can do. The most effective action will come from your and your company!

Here are a few ideas you may wish to pursue:

- Setting up a database for people wishing to car share. This could be done within your company or in association with adjacent companies.

- Provide "car sharers" with priority parking places.

- Examine the possibilities of getting together to hire a minibus.

- Consider what facilities would make walking or cycling an attractive option e.g. cycle storage facilities, changing and shower facilities, better footpath and cycle facilities.

What the Surveys show

Your questionnaires tell us how you travel to work

	Kirkton	UK(1996) average
Car	88%	70%
Bus, including minibus	10%	11%
Walk	1%	12%
Bicycle	1%	4%
Train	less than 1%	3%

These results indicate a heavy reliance on using the car to get to work with very few walking and cycling.

On the plus side, 25% of you are car passengers.

The average distance travelled to work is 9.6 miles but this varies by company depending on relocation of staff and the degree of staff specialisation.

How you get to work also relates to the length of your journey, with train users tending to travel furthest (17.5mls) followed by solo car drivers (11.4mls) and bus users (8mls). As you would expect people tend to walk the shortest distances (1ml)

Some of the solutions identified in the study

A need for:

- More reliable and frequent bus services to Kirkton Campus

- More direct bus services to reduce the need to change buses at Livingston bus station

- Cheaper fares

- More frequent and accessible train services

- Better information on bus times

- And potential for more car sharing (82% of you indicated that you would be willing to car share compared with 11% at present)

It is also noted that there is an existing level of minibus hire of 4% for journeys to and from work which tends to be very cost effective. This number could effectively be increased by encouraging people living in the same areas to get together and hire a minibus to travel to work.

One of the biggest problems is the variety of times people work on the Campus. The majority of people start about 8.00a.m and finish between 4pm and 5pm but the survey also highlights the range of times people work especially those on shift work.

It is also interesting to note that most people working on the Campus live in Livingston (44%) with 20% of people commuting from Edinburgh.

As part of the study, Napier University carried out panel interviews to get a more detailed feel for people's reasons for travelling the way they do to work, and the factors involved. The results revealed the numerous reasons why people make their travel choices and indicated that travel options could be specific and improved to and from Kirkton Campus.

The Main Aim of Travel Plan

Identify employees' travel needs and where possible, provide attractive alternatives to driving to work.

These can take the form of:

- Encouraging car sharing

- Improving public transport facilities and information

- Improving walking and cycling routes

Benefits

- You don't have to travel to or get to and from work

- You can save money (e.g. by car sharing)

- You can be healthier (walking and cycling)

- You could reduce the stress of driving to work and coping with congestion

- Retain an employers' point of view it will:

- Improve the ability to recruit the right people regardless of whether they own a car or not.

- Indicate to employees that theirs is a caring company.

- Make access to the area easier for business use and more attractive to potential customers

APPENDIX 4.3 – KIRKTON CAMPUS SENIOR MANAGEMENT INTERVIEW SCHEDULE
QUESTIONS ON GREEN COMMUTING ISSUES AT KIRKTON CAMPUS

Previous research has shown that senior management views on and support for green commuting can be vital to their success. For this reason we would like to interview you to find out your opinions on the subject, and hope that you will be able to give as full an answer as possible to the following questions:

1. Is staff travel to from and at work seen as a problem here? In what way? How serious is the (perception of) the problem.

2. What is your perception of the attempts which have been made so far to encourage greener commuting to Kirkton Campus?

3. Which measures might you consider for implementation as part of a Green Commuter Plan here? Why?

4. Can you envisage any changes in the external environment which might lead you to implement a GCP or more interventionist measures within an existing plan?

5. What barriers do you envisage to a successful GCP here?

6. Who do you think would be the key players in the development of the GCP?

7. In what ways do you think the GCP would be supported by management?

8. What influence might your organisation's business travel and company car policy have on the development of the GCP?

9. Would you be prepared to introduce financial incentives or disincentives to influence employees' mode of travel to work? Why/why not?

10. Some employers say "our responsibility to our employees begins and ends at the factory gate". Do you agree with this statement?

11. Do you think it would be important for management to lead by example in their mode of travel to work for the plan to succeed?

12. How would you describe the culture of this organisation?

13. In what ways is information circulated?

14. Are there any staff associations or trades unions which are influential at HP?

15. In your opinion has your company implemented any strategic changes in the last five years which may have affected:
    - Pay and conditions.
    - Organisational culture.
    - Organisational structure.
    - The physical environment of this worksite.
    How were these changes received?

APPENDIX 4.4 – KIRKTON CAMPUS TRAVEL SURVEY FORM

TRAVELLING TO WORK
An Employee survey

Please could you state your home postal code :

....

1. What is your Work Pattern - Usual Start / Finish Time?

Start ....   Finish ....

2. How do you usually travel to work? (Please tick one box only)

○ Bus
○ Bicycle
○ Car, on your own
○ Car, with others (car sharing)
○ Car, passenger
○ Walk
○ Motorbike
○ Train
○ Other (please specify)

....

3. How far do you travel to work?

○ Up to 1 mile
○ 1 – 2 miles
○ Over 2 miles & up to 5 miles
○ Over 5 miles & up to 10 miles
○ Over 10 miles & up to 20 miles
○ Over 20 miles

4. How long does it normally take you to get to work?

○ 0-15 minutes
○ 16-30 minutes
○ 31-60 minutes
○ Over 60 minutes

5. Which of the following would you occasionally use instead of your usual form of transport?(Please tick no more than two boxes)

○ Bus
○ Bicycle
○ Car, on your own
○ Car, with others (car sharing)
○ Car, passenger
○ Walk
○ Motorbike
○ Train
○ Other (please specify)

....

○ No alternative transport used

6. Would any of the following changes encourage you to use public transport? (If you already travel to work by public transport, which would you most like to see?) (Please tick no more than two boxes)

○ More direct bus routes
○ More frequent/reliable bus service
○ Discounted tickets/passes
○ More convenient bus stops
○ More frequent/reliable train service
○ Better service connections
○ Public transport information
○ Improved standards of transport vehicles
○ Secure Park and Ride facility
○ Other (please specify)

....

7. Would you be prepared to car-share? If so:-

○ With a colleague
○ With someone from another company nearby

PLEASE RETURN TO :
West Lothian Chamber of Commerce
The Business Centre   Almondvale Boulevard   Livingston   EH54 6QP

GREEN COMMUTER PLANS: DO THEY WORK?

The purpose of the focus group is as follows:

- To explore the reasons why people use the modes they do to get to work
- To understand the pros and cons of green commuting
- To consider whether there is any perceived need or support for green commuting at employers in Kirkton Campus

The group(s) will be tape recorded and transcribed but comments will not be attributed to any identifiable individual.

Issues to discuss

Why do you get to work in the way you do?

Is getting to work a problem? Why?

Do you think there is any need to make people's travel habits to work at Kirkton Campus "greener"? Why or why not?

Imagine trying to make your journey to work "greener". What would be the problems that this would cause you? Which of those problems are the most important?

Could your employer do anything to ease these problems? Should they?

Do you think they would help to ease these problems of getting to work? Is there any evidence that they do so in other areas of your work life?

If your manager got to work by bike or bus would it make you any more likely to do the same?

APPENDIX 5.1 – GYLE SAMPLE FOCUS GROUP SCHEDULE
OUTLINE FOCUS GROUP SCHEDULE,
GYLE – SAFEWAY

The purpose of the focus group is as follows:

- To explore the reasons why people use the modes they do to get to work
- To understand the pros and cons of green commuting
- To consider whether there is any perceived need or support for green commuting at employers in the Gyle/New Edinburgh Park

The group(s) will be transcribed but comments will not be attributed to any identifiable individual.

Issues to discuss

Why do you get to work in the way you do?

Is getting to work a problem? Why?

Do you think there is any need to make people's travel habits to work at Safeway "greener"? Why or why not?

Imagine trying to make your journey to work "greener". What would be the problems that this would cause you? Which of those problems are the most important?

Has your employer do anything to ease these problems? Should they? Should they do any more?

Do you think your employer would be prepared to help to ease these problems of getting to work? Is there any evidence that they do so in other areas of your work life?

If your manager got to work by bike or bus would it make you any more likely to do the same?

CRU RESEARCH - PUBLICATIONS LIST FROM 1999

Poor Housing and Ill Health: A Summary of Research Evidence: Housing Research Branch. (1999) (£2.50)

One Stop Shop Arrangements for Development Related Local Authority Functions: Centre for Planning Research, School of Town and Regional Planning, University of Dundee. (1999) (£5.00)
Summary available: Development Department Research Findings No.63

Research on Walking: System Three. (1999) (£5.00)

Resolving Neighbour Disputes Through Mediation in Scotland: Centre for Criminological and Legal research, University of Sheffield. (1999) (£4.00)
Summary available: Development Department Research Findings No.64

Literature Review of Social Exclusion: Centre for Urban and Regional Studies, University of Birmingham. (1999) (£5.00)

Mentally Disordered Offenders and Criminal Proceedings: Dr M Burman, Department of Sociology and Ms C Connelly, School of Law, University of Glasgow. (1999) (£7.50)

Evaluation of Experimental Bail Supervision Schemes: Ewen McCaig and Jeremy Hardin, MVA Consultancy. (1999) (£6.00)
Summary available: Social Work Research Findings No.28

An Evaluation of the 1997/98 Keep Warm This Winter Campaign: Simon Anderson and Becki Sawyer, System 3. (1999) (£5.00)
Summary available: Social Work Research Findings No.29

Attitudes to Crime, Victimisation and the Police in Scotland: A Comparison of White and Ethnic Minority Views: Jason Ditton, Jon Bannister, Stephen Farrall & Elizabeth Gilchrist`, Scottish Centre for Criminology. (1999) (£5.00)
Summary available: Crime and Criminal Justice Research Findings No.28

The Safer Cities Programme in Scotland – Evaluation of the Aberdeen (North East) Safer Cities Project: MVA. (1999) (£5.00)

Review of National Planning Policy Guidelines: Land Use Consultants. (1999) (£5.00)
Summary available: Development Department Research Findings No.65

Development Department Research Programme 1999-2000: (1999) (Free)

Environment Group Research Programme 1999-2000: (1999) (Free)

Rural Policy Research Programme 1999-2000: (1999) (Free)

Referrals between Advice Agencies and Solicitors: Carole Millar Research. (1999) (£5.00)
Summary available: Legal Studies Research Findings No.21

Life Sentence Prisoners in Scotland: Diane Machin, Nicola Coghill, Liz Levy. (1999) (£3.50)
Summary available: Crime and Criminal Justice Research Findings No.29

Report on a Conference on Domestic Violence in Scotland, Scottish Police College, Tulliallan: The Scottish Office, The Health Education Board for Scotland, The Convention of Scottish Local Authorities, The Scottish Needs Assessment Programme. (1999) (£5.00)

Making it Safe to Speak? Witness Intimidation and Protection in Strathclyde: Nicholas Fyfe, Heather McKay, University of Strathclyde. (1999) (£7.50)

Supporting Court Users: The Pilot In-Court Advice Project in Edinburgh Sheriff Court: Elaine Samuel, Department of Social Policy, University of Edinburgh. (1999) (£5.00)
Summary available: Legal Studies Research Findings No. 22

The Role of Mediation in Family Disputes in Scotland: Jane Lewis, Social and Community Planning Research. (1999) (£6.00)
Summary available: Legal Studies Research Findings No. 23

Research on Women's Issues in Scotland: An Overview: Esther Breitenbach. (1999) (Free)
Summary only available: Women's Issues Research Findings No. 1

Women in Decision-Making in Scotland: A Review of Research: Fiona Myers, University of Edinburgh. (1999) (Free)
Summary only available: Women's Issues Research Findings No. 2

Evaluation of the Debtors (Scotland) Act 1987: Study of Individual Creditors: Debbie Headrick and Alison Platts. (1999) (£5.00)
Summary available: Legal Studies Research Findings No. 10

Evaluation of the Debtors (Scotland) Act 1987: Study of Commercial Creditors: Alison Platts. (1999) (£5.00)
Summary available: Legal Studies Research Findings No. 11

Evaluation of the Debtors (Scotland) Act 1987: Study of Debtors: David Whyte. (1999) (£5.00)
Summary available: Legal Studies Research Findings No. 12

Evaluation of the Debtors (Scotland) Act 1987: Study of Facilitators: Andrew Fleming. (1999) (£5.00)
Summary available: Legal Studies Research Findings No. 13

Evaluation of the Debtors (Scotland) Act 1987: Survey of Poindings and Warrant Sales: Andrew Fleming. (1999) (£5.00)
Summary available: Legal Studies Research Findings No. 14)

Evaluation of the Debtors (Scotland) Act 1987: Survey of Payment Actions in the Sheriff Court: Andrew Fleming, Alison Platts. (1999) (£5.00)
Summary available: Legal Studies Research Findings No. 15

Evaluation of the Debtors (Scotland) Act 1987: Analysis of Diligence Statistics: Andrew Fleming, Alison Platts. (1999) (£5.00)
Summary available: Legal Studies Research Findings No. 16

Evaluation of the Debtors (Scotland) Act 1987: Overview: Alison Platts. (1999) (£5.00)

Looking After Children in Scotland: Susanne Wheelaghan, Malcolm Hill, Moira Borland, Lydia Lambert and John Triseliotis. (1999) (£5.00)
Summary available: Social Work Research Findings No.30

The Evaluation of Childrens Hearings in Scotland: Children in Focus:
Summary available: Social Work Research Findings No.31

Taking Account of Victims in the Criminal Justice System: A Review of the Literature: Andrew Sanders. (1999) (£5.00)
Summary available: Social Work Research Findings No.32

Social Inclusion Research Bulletin No.1: (1999) (Free)

Geese and their Interactions with Agriculture and the Environment: JS Kirby, M Owen and JM Rowcliffe, Wetlands Advisory Service Limited. (1999) (£10.00)
Summary available: Countryside and Natural Heritage Research Findings No.1

The Recording of Wildlife Crime in Scotland: Ed Conway, Arkleton Centre for Rural Development Research, University of Aberdeen. (1999) (£10.00)
Summary available: Countryside and Natural Heritage Research Findings No.2

Socio-Economic Benefits from Natura 2000: GF Broom, JR Crabtree, D Roberts and G Hill, Geoff Broom Associates and Macaulay Land Use Research Institute. (1999) (£5.00)
Summary available: Countryside and Natural Heritage Research Findings No.3

Crime and the Farming Community: The Scottish Farm Crime Survey 1998: Andra Laird, Sue Granville and Ruth Montgomery, George Street Research Ltd. (1999) (£10.00)
Summary available: Agricultural Policy Co-ordination and Rural Development Research Findings No.1

New Ideas in Rural Development No 7: Community Development Agents in Rural Scotland: Lynn Watkins (Rural Research Branch, The Scottish Office Central Research Unit) with Alison Brown (Scottish Community Education Council). (1999) (£2.50)
Summary available: Agricultural Policy Co-ordination and Rural Development Research Findings No.2

New Ideas in Rural Development No 8: Tackling Crime in Rural Scotland: Mary-Ann Smyth, RSK-ERA Limited. (1999) (£2.50)
Summary available: Agricultural Policy Co-ordination and Rural Development Research Findings No.3

Study of the Impact of Migration in Rural Scotland: Professor Allan Findlay, Dr David Short, Dr Aileen Stockdale (Department of Geography, University of Dundee) and Anne Findlay, Lin N Li, Lorna Philip (Department of Land Economy, University of Aberdeen). (1999) (£10.00)
Summary available: Agricultural Policy Co-ordination and Rural Development Research Findings No.4

An Electoral System for Scottish Local Government: Modelling Some Alternatives: John Curtice. (1999) (*£5.00*)

Writing for the CRU Research Series: Ann Millar, Sue Morris and Alison Platts. (1999) (*Free*)

The Effect of Closed Circuit Television on Recorded Crime Rates and Public Concern about Crime in Glasgow: Jason Ditton, Emma Short, Samuel Phillips, Clive Norris and Gary Armstrong. (1999) (*£5.00*)
Summary available: Crime and Criminal Justice Research Findings No.30

Working with Persistent Juvenile Offenders: An Evaluation of the Apex Cueten Project: David Lobley and David Smith. (1999) (*£5.00*)
Summary available: Crime and Criminal Justice Research Findings No.31

Perceptions of Local Government: A Report of Focus Group Research: Carole Millar Research. (1999) (*£5.00*)

The Role and Effectiveness of Community Councils with Regard to Community Consultation: Robina Goodlad, John Flint, Ade Kearns, Margaret Keoghan, Ronan Paddison and Mike Raco. (1999) (*£5.00*)

Supporting Parenting in Scotland: Sheila Henderson. (1999) (£5.00)
Summary available: Social Work Research Findings No.33

Investigation of Knife Stab Chararacteristics: I. Biomechanics of Knife Stab Attacks; II. Development of Body Tissue Simulant: Bioengineering Unit & Department of Mechanical Engineering, University of Strathclyde. (1999) (£5.00)

City-Wide Urban Regeneration: Lessons from Good Practice: Professor Michael Carley and Karryn Kirk (School of Planning and Housing, Heriot-Watt University). (1999) (£5.00)
Summary available: Development Department Research Findings No.66

An Examination of Unsuccessful Priority Partnership Area Bids: Peter Taylor, Ivan Turok and Annette Hastings (Department of Urban Studies, University of Glasgow). (1999) (£5.00)
Summary available: Development Department Research Findings No.67

The Community Impact of Traffic Calming Schemes: Ross Silcock Limited, Social Research Associates. (1999) (£10.00)
Summary available: Development Department Research Findings No.68

The People's Panel in Scotland: Wave 1 (June-September 1998): Dr Nuala Gormley. (1999) (Free)
Summary only: General Research Findings No.1

The People's Panel in Scotland: Wave 2 (August-November 1998): Dr Nuala Gormley. (1999) (Free)
Summary only: General Research Findings No.2

Evaluation of Prevention of Environmental Pollution from Agricultural Activity (PEPFAA) Code: Peter Evans, Market Research Scotland. (1999) (£5.00)
Summary available: General Research Findings No.3

Review of Safer Routes to School in Scotland: Derek Halden Consultancy in association with David McGuigan. (1999) (£5.00)

Climate Change: Scottish Implications Scoping Study: Andrew Kerr & Simon Allen, University of Edinburgh; Simon Shackley, UMIST; Ronnie Milne, Institute of Terrestrial Ecology. (1999) (£5.00)
Summary available: Environment Group Research Findings No.5

The Children's Traffic Club in Scotland: Katie Bryan-Brown & Gordon Harland. (1999) (£5.00)
Summary available: Development Department Research Findings No.69

An Evaluation of the New Life for Urban Scotland Initiative in Castlemilk, Ferguslie Park, Wester Hailes and Whitfield: Cambridge Policy Consultants. (1999) (£10.00)
Summary available: Development Department Research Findings No.70

National Monitoring and Interim Evaluation of the Rough Sleepers Initiative in Scotland: Anne Yanetta & Hilary Third (School of Planning & Housing, ECA/Heriot-Watt University) & Isobel Anderson (HPPU, University of Stirling). (1999) (£5.00)
Summary available: Development Department Research Findings No.71

Social Inclusion Research Bulletin No.2. (1999) (Free)

Costs in the Planning Service: Paula Gilder Consulting. (1999) (£5.00
Summary available: Development Department Research Findings No.72

Evaluation of the Teenwise Alcohol Projects: Simon Anderson & Beckie Sawyer. (1999) (£6.00)
Summary available: Crime and Criminal Justice Research Findings No.34

The Work of Precognition Agents in Criminal Cases: David J Christie & Susan R Moody (University of Dundee). (1999) (£5.00)
Summary available: Crime and Criminal Justice Research Findings No.32

Counting the Cost: Crime Against Business in Scotland: John Burrows, Simon Anderson, Joshua Bamfield, Matt Hopkins and Dave Ingram. (1999) (£10.00)
Summaries available: Crime and Criminal Justice Research Findings Nos.38, 39 and 40
Summary available: Crime and Criminal Justice Research Findings No.35

Park and Ride in Scotland: Transport Research Laboratory and Strathclyde Passenger Transport. (1999) (£5.00)
Summary available: Development Department Research Findings No.74

Evaluation of the Teenwise Alcohol Projects: Simon Anderson and Becki Sawyer. (1999) (£6.00)
Summary available: Crime and Criminal Justice Research Findings No.34

Understanding Offending Among Young People: Janet Jamieson, Gill McIvor & Cathy Murray. (1999) (£16.00)
Summary available: Social Work Research Findings No.37

The View from Arthur's Seat: A Literature Review of Housing and Support Options 'Beyond Scotland': Ken Simons & Debbie Watson (Norah Fry Research Centre, University of Bristol). (1999) (£5.00)

"If You Don't Ask You Don't Get": Review of Services to People with Learning Disabilities: The Views of People who use Services and their Carers: Kirsten Stalker, Liz Cadogan, Margaret Petrie, Chris Jones, Jill Murray (Scottish Human Services). (1999) (£5.00)

Diversion from Prosecution to Social Work and Other Service Agencies: Evaluation of the 100% Funding Pilot Programmes: Monica Barry & Gill McIvor (University of Stirling). (1999) (£5.00)
Summary available: Crime and Criminal Justice Research Findings No.37

Council Tax Collection Arrangements in Scotland and England & Wales: Institute of Revenue, Rating and Valuation. (1999) (£5.00)

Why People Don't Drive Cars: Sue Granville and Andra Laird (George Street Research). (1999) (£5.00)
Summary available: Development Department Research Findings No.75

Drug Misuse in Scotland: Simon Anderson & Martin Frischer. (2000) (£5.00)
Summary avialable: Crime and Criminal Justice Research Findings No.17

Intermediate Diets, First Diets and Agreement of Evidence in Criminal Cases: An Evaluation: Frazer McCallum & Professor Peter Duff (Aberdeen University Faculty of Law). (2000) (£5.00)
Summary available: Crime and Criminal Justice Research Findings No.42

The Experience of Violence and Harrasment of Gay Men in the City of Edinburgh: Colin Morrision & Andrew Mackay (The TASC Agency). (2000) (£5.00)
Summary available: Crime and Criminal Justice Research Findings No.41

The Development of the Scottish Partnership on Domestic Abuse and Recent Work in Scotland: Dr Shelia Henderson (Reid Howie Associates). (2000) (£5.00)

Children, Young People and Crime in Britain and Ireland: From Exclusion to Inclusion –1998 Conference Papers: Monica Barry (University of Stirling), Joe Connolly (Action for Children), Olwyn Burke, Dr J Curran (Central Research Unit, Scottish Executive). (2000) (£5.000)

Overview of Written Evidence Received as Part of the Review of the Public Health Function in Scotland :
Summary available only: General Research Finding No.4

Assessment of the Voter Education Campaign for the Scottish Parliament Elections: (Scotland Office Publication): Andra Laird, Sue Granville & Jo Fawcett (George Street Research). (2000) (£5.00)

Review of the Experience of Community Councils as Statutory Consultees on Planning Applications: Ewan McCraig, MVA. (2000) (£5.00)
Summary Available Development Department Research Findings No.77

Family Support and Community Care: A Study of South Asian Older People: Alison Bowes and Naira Dar with the assistance of Archana Srivastava (University of Stirling). (2000) (£6.00)

An Evaluation of the SACRO (Fife) Young Offender Mediation Project: Becki Sawyer, System 3. (2000) (£5.00)
Summary available: Crime and Criminal Justice Research Findings No.43

Development Department Research 2000-2001: (2000) (Free)

Environment Group Research Programme 2000-2001: (2000) (Free)

Social Inclusion Bulletin No.3: (2000) (Free)

Road Safety in the Scottish Curriculum: Tony Graham, ODS Ltd. (2000) (£5.00)
Summary available: Development Department Research Findings No.78

The Role of Information and Communications Technology in Road Safety Education: BITER – The British Institute of Traffic Education Research. (2000) (£5.00)
Summary available: Development Department Research Findings No.79

Evaluation of Scottish Road Safety Campaign Travel Packs: Sharon Reid, Andra Laird & Jo Fawcett. (2000) (£5.00)
Summary available: Development Department Research Findings No.82

Audit of ICT Initiatives: In Social Inclusion Partnerships and Working for Communities Pathfinders in Scotland: Joanna Gilliatt, Doug Maclean & Jenny Brogden, Lambda Research & Consultancy Ltd. (2000) (£5.00)

Researching Ethnic Minorities in Scotland: Reid-Howie Associates. (2000) (Free)

A Comparative Evaluation of Greenways and Conventional Bus Lanes: Colin Buchanan and Partners. (2000) (£5.00)
Summary available: Development Department Research Findings No.83

Advertising Planning Proposals: James Barr Planning Consultants. (2000) (£5.00)
Summary available: Development Department Research Findings No.84

The Role of Pre-Application Discussions and Guidance in Planning: Peter Gibson and Robert Stevenson, The Customer Managerment Consultancy Ltd. (2000) (£5.00)
Summary available: Development Department Research Findings No.85

Developing Markets for Recyclable Materials in Scotland: Prioritising Materials: Enviros RIS Ltd in association with Clean Washington Centre. (2000) (Free).
Summary only available: Environment Group Research Findings No.6

The Development of the Scottish Partnership on Domestic Abuse and recent Work in Scotland: Dr S Henderson, Reid Howie Associates. (2000) (£5.00).

Evaluation of the Airborne Initiative (Scotland): Gill McIvor, Vernon Gayle, Kirstina Moodie, Stirling University and Ann Netten, University of Kent. (2000) (£5.00)
Summary available: Crime and Criminal Justice Research Finding No.45

A Review of the Research Literature on Serious and Sexual Offenders: Clare Connelly and Shanti Williamson, University of Glasgow. (2000) (£8.00).
Summary available: Crime and Criminal Justice Research Finding No.46

The Quality of Services in Rural Scotland: Steven Hope, Simon Anderson and Becki Sawyer, System Three.
Summary available: Rural Affairs Research Finding No.5.

Social Exclusion in Rural Areas; A Literature Review and Conceptual Framework: Mark Shuckshank and Lorna Philip, University of Aberdeen. (2000) (£10).
Summary available: Rural Affairs Research Finding No.6.

Charities Report:
1. **Scottish Charity Legislation; Full Report** (2000) (£15.00).
2. **Scottish Charity Legislation; Executive Summary** (2000) (Free).
3. **Scottish Charity Legislation; Annexes** (2000) (£5.00).
4. **Public Charitable Collections** (2000) (£5.00).
5. **Public Trusts and Educational Endowments** (2000) (£5.00).
University of Dundee.
Summary available: Legal Studies Research Finding 26

Meeting in the Middle: A Study of Solicitors' and Mediators Divorce Practice: Fiona Myers and Fran Wasoff. University of Edinburgh. (2000) (£5.00)
Summary available: Legal Studies Research Finding No.25.

Real Burdens: Survey of Owner Occupiers' Understanding of Title Conditions: Andra Laird and Emma Peden, George Street Research (2000) (£5.00)
Summary available: Legal Studies Research Finding No.27

Survey of Complainers to the Scottish Legal Services Ombudsman: The Customer Management Consultancy Ltd (2000) (£5.00)

An Evaluation of Electronically Monitored Restriction of Liberty Orders: David Lobley and David Smith, Lancaster University. (2000) (£5.00)
Summary available: Crime and Criminal Justice Research Finding No.47

Interviewing and Drug Testing of Arrestees in Scotland: A Pilot Study of the Arrestee Drug Abuse Monitoring (ADAM) Methodology: Neil McKeganey, Clare Connelly, Lesley Reid & John Norrie University of Glasgow, Janusz Knepil Gartnavel General Hospital Glasgow. (2000) (£5.00)
Summary available: Crime and Criminal Justice Research Finding No 48

The Role of Pre-Application Discussions and Guidance in Planning: Peter Gibson and Robert Stevenson, The Customer Management Consultancy Ltd. (2000) (£5.00)
Summary available: Development Department Research Finding No 85

The Role of Sport in Regenerating Deprived Areas: Fred Coalter with Mary Allison and John Taylor, Centre for Lesisure Research. (2000) (£5.00)
Summary available: Development Department Research Finding No 86

"Huts and Hutters" in Scotland: Research Consultancy Services. (2000) (£5.00)

Motivations to Public Service: Sue Granville and Andra Laird, George Street Research. (2000) (Free)
Summary only available: Development Department Research Findings No.87

The What, Where and When of Being a Councillor: Paolo Vestri and Stephen Fitzpatrick, Scottish Local Government Information Unit. (2000) (Free)
Summary only available: Development Department Research Findings No.88

Further information on any of the above is available by contacting:

Dr A Scott
Chief Research Officer
Scottish Executive Central Research Unit
Room J1-5
Saughton House
Broomhouse Drive
Edinburgh
EH11 3XA

or by accessing the World Wide Website: www.scotland.gov.uk